Simone Francescato, Roberta Maierhofer,
Valeria Minghetti, Eva-Maria Trinkaus (eds.)
Senior Tourism

Aging Studies | Volume 13

The series **Aging Studies** is edited by Heike Hartung, Ulla Kriebernegg and Roberta Maierhofer.

SIMONE FRANCESCATO, ROBERTA MAIERHOFER,
VALERIA MINGHETTI, EVA-MARIA TRINKAUS (EDS.)

Senior Tourism
Interdisciplinary Perspectives on Aging and Traveling

[transcript]

This book was published with the financial support of the Department of Linguistics and Comparative Cultural Studies, Ca' Foscari University of Venice.

Ca' Foscari
University
of Venice
**Department of Linguistics
and Comparative
Cultural Studies**

The printing of this book was supported by the University of Graz and the Center for Inter-American Studies.

Bibliographic information published by the Deutsche Nationalbibliothek
The Deutsche Nationalbibliothek lists this publication in the Deutsche Nationalbibliografie; detailed bibliographic data are available in the Internet at http://dnb.d-nb.de

© 2017 transcript Verlag, Bielefeld

All rights reserved. No part of this book may be reprinted or reproduced or utilized in any form or by any electronic, mechanical, or other means, now known or hereafter invented, including photocopying and recording, or in any information storage or retrieval system, without permission in writing from the publisher.

Cover concept: Kordula Röckenhaus, Bielefeld
Cover illustration: © Prof. Roberta Maierhofer, Graz, 2017
Typeset by Justine Buri, Bielefeld
Printed by Majuskel Medienproduktion GmbH, Wetzlar
Print-ISBN 978-3-8376-3703-8
PDF-ISBN 978-3-8394-3703-2

Contents

Editors' Introduction | 7

New Options for Senior Tourism
Literary Tours and Albania
Ilda Erkoçi | 19

"Almost Fatally Disoriented"
Tourism and Aging in Moritz Thomsen's *The Saddest Pleasure*
Simone Francescato | 33

"A Man Should Be Able to Take a Trip if He Wants"
Senior Tourism in Oscar Casares' *Amigoland*
Ulla Kriebernegg | 49

**(Un)Comfortably Moving Out of the Comfort Zone:
Life as Travel**
Roberta Maierhofer | 77

Senior Tourism and Accessibility
Evolving trends and implications for the travel and tourism industry
Valeria Minghetti | 97

**Undermining Retirement as Leisure Time
in Deborah Moggach's *These Foolish Things* and
Its Film Adaptation *The Best Exotic Marigold Hotel***
Maricel Oro-Piqueras | 121

The Older You Are, the More Sustainable You Get
A Sociological Snapshot of Cultural Tourism at an Eastern Adriatic "Living Heritage Site"
Mirko Petrić, Ivan Puzek, Inga Tomić-Koludrović | 139

Never Too Late to Remember
Cruising the Past in Paule Marshall's *Praisesong for the Widow*
Anna Scacchi | 167

Cruising To Be Young Again
The Mystification of Senior Tourism in *Love Boat*
Cinzia Schiavini | 191

Contributors | 207

Editors' Introduction

Over the past century, tourism has grown to be a defining trait of contemporary society, both from an economic and a cultural perspective. As a major industry worldwide, tourism has recently come to represent a strategic sector for the overcoming of the present economic crisis. As a social practice, tourism has long been recognized as central for the construction of cultural identity and heritage within a highly interconnected world where mobility is, for better or worse, constantly increasing.

Mobility is also increasing among the elderly. In the Western countries, in particular, longer life expectancy and the growth of aging populations, with their consequent involvement in both productive and non-productive (recreational) activities, demand new and serious consideration of post-retirement mobility not only in our era but beyond. No longer considered as an inactive period, post-retirement has now become, as Tongren suggests, "a stage in life when a person can do any number of things that have been put off for years and travel is a major element in most retirement plans" (qtd in Gibson 11). In the tourist market, "elderly" or "senior" tourists have started to be considered as a particularly valuable resource among the rest of the tourist population. In Europe, for instance, senior tourists have lately attracted the attention of the European Commission, and, more in general, of public and private tourist operators, not only for their economic contribution to local tourism development, but also for seniors' preference to travel in low and medium seasons, which helps reducing tourism pressure in peak periods, especially in most popular destinations (EC 2014).

But elderly people also travel for reasons that well extend beyond the commonly accepted understanding of leisure travel. In an age of globally extended (work) mobility, for instance, many of them engage in what Lago and Poffley have called "multigenerational travel" [1] (Gibson 13), in which they visit their children and grandchildren who temporarily or permanently reside away from them. While they do so, they also have the chance and time to getting to know unknown places and cultures, like 'intentional' tourists do. Travel and tourism, thus, come to play a key role in intergenerational dialogue and in the preservation of family ties.[2] Promoting this dialogue however requires the removal of many existing physical and socio-cultural barriers (accessibility, transportation, information, health care, etc.) that hamper some seniors to travel (EC 2014).

Although "travel" and "aging" are concepts that have enjoyed significant semantic overlapping in intellectual history, their actual association has always encountered resistance. In one of the founding texts of aging studies, *The Journey of Life* (1992), Thomas J. Cole has identified travel as the most important metaphor ever used to describe the process of aging from the ancient times to the present. But whereas aging is commonly accepted as some kind of journey, the reverse equation is problematic. What is normally associated with mobility and travel (youth, health, enjoyment, open-minded-

---

1 | "Multigenerational holiday" also means seniors traveling with their relatives or with grandchildren only. This is rapidly increasing at international level, given the evolution in household composition (rise in divorces, more 'second' and 'third' families, etc.) and the development of a vertical family model (less children and more grandparents or aunts/uncles per child) (EC 2010).

2 | "Rootedness" and "mobility" also interact significantly in heritage tourism, an ever-growing phenomenon where travel is motivated by a need to recover as much as possible of one's forgotten ancestry, something to which the present book pays particular attention. Another aspect which should be taken into account in mobility studies in the next years is the number of elderly migrants in the huge recent flows from the Middle East to Europe.

ness) is often perceived as antithetical to the distinguishing features of late life (illness, closure, rootedness, clinging to one's old habits). As a result, late-life mobility, even in the socially acceptable form of senior tourism—stands out as a sort of oxymoron, something which ultimately exposes the ageist bias of our society, where the elderly is supposed to enjoy very low exposure to travel. Thus a paradox is apparent.

The recent thriving of senior tourism shown by statistics calls for a reassessment of these issues that reaches beyond the merely economic. What are the social and cultural effects of such a rising trend for the elderly? Should we take it as a convincing evidence of the empowerment of the elderly, at least in our Western world?

One thing seems to be sure: senior tourism is a complex phenomenon that deserves a much broader contextualization than the one provided only by quantitative studies in the field (Gibson 2002; Nimrod 2008; Sedgley et al. 2011). Senior tourism cannot be isolated and analyzed simply as a segment of the whole tourist market, as this simplified approach would suppress important aspects related to the particularity of the subjects involved *and* their individual experience of it. It is not by chance that leisure travel for the elderly population often represents a rite of passage, associated with retirement, and thus strongly related to an opening up of possibilities and a personal growth (Gibson 11).

This volume aims to bridge the disciplinary gap between tourism studies and aging studies by investigating the intersections of tourism and aging from a variety of perspectives which focus on the many ways in which senior tourism is socially constructed and/or individually experienced. We agree on the fact that the extant research on tourism is still largely quantitative and would benefit from an interdisciplinary exchange with *qualitative-oriented* research. So far, quantitative research has not provided a comprehensive and exhaustive picture of the phenomenon, whose very 'subjects' are often very difficult to pinpoint. As Patterson observes, since the segment of the aging population is changing over time, the term "senior tourists" often applies un-problematically to cohort of people sometimes separated by forty years, for whom it is impossible to get to a determinate clear-cut tourist typologies (Patterson 12-3).

There is a need to understand not only the possible economic advantages of encouraging tourism in old age, but also *whether* such trend is going to undermine in the long run stereotypes and biased perceptions regarding the elderly population—in line with the international agenda of the active aging movement—and perhaps also determine a redefinition of the overall idea of leisure travel. This is where the contribution of a humanist-oriented approach comes into play. Both critical gerontology and cultural analysis insist in fact on a radical shift of the object of investigation from "external truth" to a world of "constructed reality" (Sedgley 426), which would allow space for analyzing issues not commonly associated with senior tourism.

The following essays prove that the intersections of tourism and aging are many and still to be tackled. They range from the socio-economic aspects of post-retirement travel to the representations of the traveling elderly in literature, film and media, and the influence of travel on late-life creativity. These contributions engage in a multi- and interdisciplinary research, which significantly expands groundbreaking works like Patterson's *Growing Older: Tourism and Leisure Behaviour of Older Adults* (2006), substantial chapters in Buhalis & Darcy's *Accessible Tourism* (2010) and Buhalis, Darcy, Ambrose's *Best Practice in Accessible Tourism: Inclusion, Disability, Ageing Population and Tourism* (2012)—which have drawn attention to senior tourism as a distinct subject of investigation. They also answer Diane Sedgley et al. (2011)'s reasonable plea for the necessity of a humanist approach to such subject.

The essays are ordered alphabetically and resort to (and fruitfully combine) a variety of theoretical and methodological resources. The volume opens with "New Options for Senior Tourists: Literary Tours in Albania" by Ilda Erkoçi, an essay that examines the relevance of literary tourism for the elderly population. This essay argues, in line with current data, that while reflecting attitudes commonly associated to late life like escapism and nostalgia, literary tourism has also effects on the possibility of socialization and new experience for elderly tourists. Her essay also offers itself as a short introduction to literary tourism in Albania, a very recent and expanding industry.

The second essay, "'Almost Fatally Disoriented': Tourism and Aging in Moritz Thomsen's *The Saddest Pleasure*" by Simone Francescato explores the relations between aging, travel, and memory in the autobiographical memoir *The Saddest Pleasure: A Journey on Two Rivers* (1990) by American expatriate, former Peace Corps member, and travel writer Moritz Thomsen (1915-1991). Thomsen lived for more than two decades as a poor man in a small town in Ecuador, where he helped a local black man to establish and run his own farm. Forced to retire by his work partner and suffering from poor health, the solitary 63-year-old writer living in Quito decided to embark on a long-dreamt tourist trip to Brazil as a means to overcome his existential despair. Drawing from classic studies on aging (Cole 1992; Woodward 1991) as well as recent studies on the relations between aging and narrative (De Falco, 2010), Francescato argues that Thomsen's narrative significantly deconstructs our commonly accepted notion of 'post-retirement leisure trip,' while debunking the protagonist's 'tourist gaze' and his exoticist fantasies about Brazil. The representation of other elderly tourists in this book is read in the light of Thomsen's struggle with his own self-idealization and denial of aging.

Ulla Kriebernegg's essay "A Man Should Be Able to Take a Trip if He Wants: Senior Tourism in Oscar Casares's *Amigoland*" discusses senior tourism in the context of the increasingly popular genre of "nursing home escape narratives"—a genre in which nursing home residents escape the specter of long-term residential care in order to embark on journeys that prove life-altering. By means of Oscar Casares' first novel *Amigoland* (2009), Kriebernegg looks at how the care home escape novel uses features of the road movie and discusses how mobility, space, and place inform an old man's identity construction as he embarks on a journey from the USA to Mexico to find his peace of mind.

Representations of travel and mobility are important cultural narratives expressing issues and concerns of postmodern identity. By juxtaposing Vilém Flusser's concept of the *expelled* and Zygmunt Bauman's notions of *pilgrim, stroller, vagabond,* and *tourist,* in "(Un)Comfortably Moving Out of the Comfort Zone: Life as Travel" Roberta Maierhofer investigates movements through space and time within a life course as expressions of conscious acts of appropriation, where travel can express the matrix of time and experience, and how by the narration of these experiences of travel an escape can be enabled—to use Bauman's words—from the limits that each society sets to "life strategies that can be imagined." The narrative reflections of changed spaces and strange contexts allow for an expression of the fluidity of one's identity, and thus open up possibilities of moving beyond defined positions of self. If identity is defined by both continuity and change over a life course, the importance is to narrate one's life in an on-going process of dialogue between the strange and the familiar. Such reflections are used to reflect on the quest for individual identity as related to travel and aging in American literature and to analyze in particular Grace Paley's short story "The Long Distance Runner" (1974) and, more extensively, the novel *Praisesong for the Widow* (1983) by African American writer Paule Marshall.

Valeria Minghetti's essay, "Senior Tourism and Accessibility: Evolving Trends and Key Issues", examines senior tourism by focusing on aging, disability and accessibility as three high-interrelated concepts. The current evolution of senior population and the extent to which an increase in life expectancy corresponds to a greater physical and psychological wellbeing have important consequences on seniors' consumption behavior and on the possibility of accessing and enjoying specific products and services, also in tourism. Starting from a discussion on the various definitions of "seniors" and on the characteristics of main senior tourism market segments, her essay focuses attention on how the tourism industry and destinations can model their supply in order to ensure easy access to information and tourist services for elderly tourists, also through the use of Information and Communication Technologies (ICTs). In particular, the role of technological innovation in reducing information barriers and supporting social inclusion is analyzed. The interoperability among tourism operators; the integration of tourism- and accessibility-related information; the customization of contents and, finally, the implementation of Accessible Design principles, all of which can represent crucial aspects to develop an inclusive tourism approach.

In "Undermining Retirement as Leisure Time in Deborah Moggach's *These Foolish Things* and its film adaptation *The Best Exotic Marigold Hotel*" Maricel Oró-Piqueras focuses on cultural representation of senior tourism and on the process of adaptation from text to film. In particular she concentrates on how the idealized representation of happy old age of the baby-boomers generation is exploited by the tourism industry in order to acquire new customers. In Moggach's novel (2004) and its film version (2012) a group of British citizens move to a retirement hotel in Bangalore, India, in order to escape a present and future situation which they perceive as limiting and suffocating. By leaving behind their British contexts, the older characters discover that the concept "old age" does not need to be limiting; rather, it is our culture which limits it. Thus, they also discover other facets of themselves which are more romanticised in the film version than in the novel. Still, both succeed in bringing to the surface the incongruities of stereotypical images of retirement and old age within Western society by pointing out at their complex nature.

The essay by Mirko Petrić, Ivan Puzek and Inga Tomić-Koludrović is a brief case study of how tourists perceived as "aging" can help sustain the essential qualities of what has recently been described as "living heritage sites". Its aim is to serve as a relational contextual explanation grounded in one concrete example, which Jack Levine refers to as "sociological snapshots". This particular snapshot was taken in a well-known heritage center on the Eastern Adriatic coast, inscribed on UNESCO's World Heritage List as "the historical complex of Split with the Palace of Diocletian" in 1979. Following a brief overview of the development of tourism on the Eastern Adriatic coast, as well as a discussion of specific heritage qualities of the historical core of Split, the results of two comprehensive surveys of tourists visiting the site (carried out in 2005 and 2013) are presented and compared. The discussion of the sociodemographic data and motivations to travel of the types of tourists obtained by means of cluster analysis suggests that experientially-oriented and culturally sensitive tourists aged 50 and over are presently best suited to the purpose of maintaining the heritage qualities of the "living site" in question. The text concludes with questions about how the process is going to develop in the future, when the currently younger visitors, with different educational background, cultural interests, and financial means will also "begin to age".

In "Never Too Late for Remembering: Cruising the Past in Paule Marshall's Praisesong for the Widow" Anna Scacchi examines, like Maierhofer, Marshall's classic novel of late-life travel, but reads the text within the context of an increasingly marketized experience of African American history. Prompted by the famous TV series Roots, in the last three decades American heritage tourism to the West African shores has become big business, being advertised as a way for black Americans to "rediscover" their African roots and heal the wounds inflicted by the trauma of slavery. Such tours exploit the emotional impact of the memory of slavery on contemporary middle-class black Americans, while providing sentimentalized experiences with a happy ending. Marshall's 1983 novel, on the contrary, depicts a very different kind of travel experience where the protagonist ultimately succeeds in recovering a connection, formerly dismissed as odd and atavistic, with her ancestors which leads her to engage in political and cultural change back home. By recovering her links with the ancestors and the black Diaspora in the Americas, the 64-year-old Avey Johnson discovers a new strategy of survival in racist United States.

In the essay "Cruising to Be Young Again: The Mystification of Senior Tourism in *Love Boat*," which concludes this collection, Cinzia Schiavini investigates the cultural representations and misrepresentations of old age in one of the most popular leisure activities for old people: cruise ship tourism. She focuses in particular on *Love Boat*, a popular TV series of the Seventies and Eighties, which transformed cruise ship tourism in an affordable and tempting fantasy vacation for middle-class consumers. Drawing from contemporary tourism studies, Schiavini postulates that cruise ship tourism constitutes in the popular imagination the convergence between the "romantic" and the "collective" gazes contemporary tourism relies on. She also argues that cruise ship tourism, due to its intrinsic features, has been one of the most powerful agent in the domestication and commodification of the exotic, to make it usable especially to aged people. Her essay explores to what extent the socially affable captain, the all-American crew, the abundance of single people aboard looking for love, and a setting where passengers are indulged in opulence and luxury, rejuvenate and distort the reality of cruise ship tourism, and thus the impact of the third age in American contemporary society.

This volume is the result of the international conference held at the University of Venice Ca' Foscari in January 2014, during which a group of scholars from different disciplines and from various European universities came together to engage in an exchange of ideas and methodologies. The conference was organized by the Department of Linguistics and Comparative Cultural Studies (Ca' Foscari), in collaboration with the Department of Economics (Ca' Foscari), C.I.S.E.T. (International Centre for Studies on Tourism Economics), and ENAS (European Network of Aging Studies), whose founder, Roberta Maierhofer (University of Graz, Austria) provided the keynote lecture. The conference also included contributions by Flavio Gregori, Danilo Cavapozzi and Francesca Zantomio (Ca' Foscari) and also by Enrico Capiozzo and Lisa Danese, CEO and Content and Community Manager of VEASYT Srl, a research spin-off of Ca' Foscari University aiming to develop skills in the field of language and sensorial accessibility. Over the years we have received support from all the contributors and positive feedback by those who kindly sponsored this event. In publishing some of the revised papers delivered during the conference, we do hope to contribute to redefine any restricted notion of senior tourism, and to re-conceptualize it as a complex phenomenon associated with important economic, social, and cultural changes, which may inspire future research on the subject.

WORKS CITED

Buhalis, Dimitrios, and Simon Darcy, eds. *Accessible tourism: Concepts and Issues.* Vol. 45. Bristol: Channel View Publications, 2011. Print.

Buhalis, Dimitrios, Simon Darcy, and Ivor Ambrose, eds. *Best Practice in Accessible Tourism:Inclusion, Disability, Ageing Population and Tourism.* Vol. 53. Bristol: Channel View Publications, 2012. Print.

Cole, Thomas R. *The Journey of Life: A Cultural History of Aging in America.* Cambridge MA: Cambridge University Press, 1992. Print.

European Commission (EC). "Europe the best destination for Seniors", Draft Report,Enterprise and Industry Directorate General, Services Industry Tourism Policy, September 2014, EB: http://ec.europa.eu/DocsRoom/documents/6924/attachments/1/translations/en/reditions/pdf

Gibson, Heather J. "Busy travelers: Leisure-travel patterns and meanings in later life." *World Leisure Journal,* 44.2 (2002): 11-20.

Lago, Dan, and James Kipp Poffley. "The aging population and the hospitality industry in2010: Important trends and probable services." *Journal of Hospitality & Tourism Research* 17.1 (1993): 29-47.

Nimrod, Galit. "Retirement and tourism themes in retirees' narratives." *Annals of Tourism Research* 35.4 (2008): 859-78.

Patterson, Ian R. *Growing Older: Tourism and Leisure Behaviour of Older Adults.* Wallingford, Oxfordshire, UK: CABI Pub, 2006. Print.

Sedgley, Diane, Annette Pritchard, and Nigel Morgan. "Tourism and Ageing: A Transformative Research Agenda." *Annals of Tourism Research* 38.2 (2011): 422-36.

Tongren, Hale N. "Travel Plans of the Over-65 Market Pre and Post-retirement." *Journal of Travel Research* 19.2 (1980): 7-11.

WHO, The Global Movement for Active Aging. Web. http://www.unsystem.org/scn/archives/scnnews19/ch27.htm

New Options for Senior Tourism
Literary Tours and Albania

Ilda Erkoçi

Introduction

Senior tourism is a growing industry not only because of the money it generates, but also because it does so outside the high season.[1]

A quick online navigation reveals that there are plenty of trips exclusively designed for the elderly. They provide a wide variety of destinations and exotic adventures off the beaten track in many countries. ElderTreks, for instance, offers "wildlife and tribal African safaris, active hiking trips to the Rockies, Himalayas and Andes, expeditions by icebreakers to the Arctic and Antarctic and cultural journeys throughout Asia, South America and much of the world." (ElderTreks)

Currently most of these trips are limited to the EU citizens and countries. One has to "be resident in one of the European Union countries" ("Tourism for Seniors"), which is a discriminating condition. It is good that the Senior Tourism Initiative was launched

---

1 | The contribution of senior citizens to the European tourism industry is indeed significant and should be reinforced to face the challenge of seasonality, stimulating economic growth and jobs in Europe. Senior citizens (with 55 years old and over) represent around 25% of the European population. They have both purchasing power and leisure time (mainly in the retirement age), thus representing a significant economic market potential. ("Tourism for Seniors")

by the European Commission in 2012 to increase travel by the senior sector in Europe, but it does not take account of the fact that Albanian citizens, for example, no longer need a visa to travel to EU countries, and as such, it is high time the initiative extended to include additional countries. Off-the-track regions may have a lot of unexploited and unknown development potential.

In addition, few of these companies consider the possibility of focusing on an interest in literature. Surely, they should, given that this group is the one that is most likely to truly appreciate literary tourism, not only because of the time available, but also because its members often possess the appropriate cultural (literary) background and experience.

What is literary tourism?

Anyone who likes reading books has probably experienced the moment when you close your eyes and wonder what the place you have just been reading about may look like. Is it inspired by the author's environs, his home town or travels or is it pure fiction? There is an easy way to find out—literary tourism. Instead of going to the seaside for your holiday, pack your backpack and set out for a trip to places where William Shakespeare or Charles Dickens wrote their major works, visit the favourite spots of the Beatniks or the grave of Ernest Hemingway and search for the connections between what you have read and what you get to see. (tourismreview.com)

Literary tourism can have two distinct emphases: both the places associated with the particular authors, and the settings of either their poetry or novels. This may include following the itinerary of a fictional character in a novel, visiting settings from a story or tracking down the haunts of a novelist. Scholars Robinson and Andersen who have researched the links between literature and tourism, believe that tourists want to visit the writers' homes as a way of "connecting with the space where great books came into being, walk where the writers walked, see what the writers saw." (18) Ireland, for instance, is nowadays one of the major nations using its literary heritage to promote cultural tourism:

Dublin is a tale, a story, a legend, a dialogue—it is itself a conversation, ongoing, inclusive and invigorating with literature as an essential element of its composition. Literature is a major contributor to the city's cultural, social, intellectual and economic life and continually enriches the experiences of visitors and inhabitants alike. (Dublin UNESCO)

Nicola Watson, a fervent scholar of literary tourism explains that "in order to become a literary tourist you only need a novel and an inquisitive mind-set; however, there are literary guides, literary maps, and literary tours to help you on your way." (9) To put this in the above context, Dublin is particularly associated with the Bloomsday festival which gathers tourists from all over the world on the anniversary of the day on which James Joyce set the action of his novel Ulysses.

Literary tourism is in a way a materialization of literature which allows one to give a new substance to the often elusive experience of reading. It makes literature more tangible by providing a touch of the real. After all, the very reason why people set off on literary tourism is to seek real people, objects and places, to anchor and perhaps inhabit for a while the worlds they have approached through reading. "Dull of spirit would s/he be who did not get more out of literature from experiencing it with their feet" says John Sutherland. He adds that "literature always seems richer when you visit the place that inspired it." (The Guardian) A similar feeling can also be even evoked from the ancient world:

Our emotions are somehow stirred in those places in which the feet of those whom we love and admire have trodden. Wherefore even Athens delights us not so much through its magnificent buildings and its exquisite works of ancient art as through the memory of its great men: 'twas here they dwelt, 'twas here they sat, 'twas here they engaged in their philosophical discussions. And with reverence I contemplate their tombs. (Cicero, *Laws*, No 2)

A literary tour to just one spot can sometimes do more than several trips to various places:

We rode through the countryside in a 16-passenger bus seeking the locations of Hardy's novels and poems. In the Stinsford churchyard, where Hardy's heart is buried—the rest of him is under the floor in Westminster Abbey—we read aloud the poems about the dead. Like countless literary pilgrims before us, we stood in the village church at West Stafford where Tess married Angel ... We ate box lunches on the lawn of the gabled house Hardy used as Bathsheba's farmhouse. *And none of us has ever seen Hardy or his writings quite the same way again.* (Maltby 2, my italics)

As the last sentence of the paragraph suggests, an additional benefit of literary tourism is that it can motivate a better appreciation and understanding of literature.

Literary tourism and senior tourism

Literary tourism is not age exclusive. Anyone at any time may find some inspiration to follow the footsteps of one's favourite writer. Yet, literary tourism and senior tourism do share some features which might not seem obvious at first glance.

First, escapism. Escapism is a major motivation for senior tourism.[2] Seniors might choose to go on literary tourism as it can offer an uncommon way to break off with daily routines in search of an exciting experience. As literary tourists often do, seniors might want to deliberately obscure the boundary between fiction and real life, attempting to become physically closer to the imaginary narrated world:

---

2 | Cf Cleaver et al (1999), Stone and Nichol (1999), You & O'Leary (1999, Shoemaker (2000), Muller and O'Cass (2001), Hsu et al (2007). See table 1: Summary of Main Studies on Senior Tourists' Motivation from 1999 to 2010 in Girish Prajag "Senior Travelers' Motivations And Future Behavioral Intentions: The Case Of Nice". *Journal of Travel & Tourism Marketing*, 29: 665-681, 2012.

I guess I wanted a world as filled with sound and fury as Faulkner's, as cradled in promises and dark mysteries as Frost's, as populated with oddballs and heroes as Steinbeck's. I wanted the mountains and the sea, the brutal winters that froze desire, and the unchanging tropical heat that fed a lazy anticipation .... I wanted the violent awakenings of O'Connor's Georgia as well. In books and legends these worlds existed for me, but I wondered whether, if I stepped beyond the magical circle of imagining, these worlds would disappear like a mirage shimmering into memory. (Pearson 4)

What is special about literature is that it can present the reader-tourist with visits off the usual tourist tracks. Of course, there are exceptions as is the case of Shakespeare's Stratford or Austen's Bath, yet, most literary places are not typically overrun by massive tourists of all ages, which may benefit seniors.

Next, nostalgia. Several senior tourism scholars[3] emphasize nostalgia among the senior tourists' travel motivations, which is a very typical feature of literary tourism, too. This group of tourists may be drawn to literary places for some broader and deeper connection than the specific writer or the story, such as nostalgia for the past as described in books or memories linked with childhood: "I wanted the perfect memory of childhood that Hannibal[4] represented." (Pearson 4)

In addition, literary tourism can also meet other travel motivations highlighted by senior tourism studies such as relaxation and socialization alongside the literary experience. It can complement the travel experience in a way different from the other arts which have long been a conventional aspect of tourism.

As aesthetic cultural tourism, literary tourism is distinctive. Literature (prose, fiction, poetry and drama) is not like other art forms. Unlike the

---

3 | Cf Cleaver et al (1999), Muller and O'Cass (2001), Huang and Tsai (2003), Sellick (2004), etc. See footnote 2.
4 | Mark Twain's boyhood home and also setting for the adventures of Tom Sawyer and Huck Finn.

visual arts and music, literature can potentially be engaged with at a personal level by anybody who can read and understands the conventions used by the author in telling a story or arranging words to create aesthetic and semantic patterns. The author and the reader are closer to sharing the art, you might say, than the sculptor or ceramic artist and their audience. (Robinson and Andersen xiv)

Of course, readers of any age might appreciate this kind of tourism, but seniors are more likely to be engaged with a reading culture and have an appetite for long books and even poetry that younger travelers do not usually share.

Herbert has found that the majority of the people visiting Chawton and Laugharne (connected respectively with Jane Austen and Dylan Thomas) were in their fifties and sixties (321) which is a clear indication that there is literary interest from this specific age group. What seems important to consider is organization. While a few seniors may organize trips privately, there are certainly advantages to having a planned tour, which would not only minimize risks and make the journey more comfortable, but also encourage sharing and enhancing the experience.

THE CASE FOR ALBANIA

Actually, tourism in Albania is still in its infancy, and some might say it is not ready to be part of the global market. Yet, with some help it can be possible. Situated in the heart of the Mediterranean, on the Adriatic and Ionian Seas, Albania is a country rich in natural beauties having remained relatively free from exploitation. It offers a wide variety of sites including sandy beaches (the Riviera) as well as rocky mountains (the Alps). But the country is also rich in cultural heritage, including a distinct literary legacy. Its long history dating back to Illyrian, Greek and Roman civilizations is reflected in well-preserved ruins and other treasures. Albania is home to three World Heritage cities: Butrint, Berat and Gjirokastër.

In the foreword to *Shqipëria dhe shqiptarët në vepra të piktorëve të huaj* (*Albania and the Albanians in world art*), Ismail Kadare writes: "Although Albania was forgotten by states and rulers, European art did not forget it. Byron, Vivaldi, Delacroix and dozens of other famous artists continued their search for original themes in the events, sounds and colours of this land." (Hudhri 8) Ferid Hudhri has recorded 140 international painters (a considerable number for a small country like Albania) who have made Albania or the Albanians subject of their work. His study reveals that in some of the best-known museums of the world—the Historical Museum of Vienna, the Louvre Gallery in Paris, the British Museum in London, the Gallery of Modern Art in Rome, the Palace of Doge in Venice, the Brooklyn Gallery in New York, the Benaki Museum in Athens, the Tetriakov Gallery in Moscow and many more, even in faraway Japan hundreds of paintings, portraits, landscapes, etchings, lithographs and sculptures on Albanian subjects can be found. Edward Lear, Edith Durham, Eugéne Delacroix, Léon Cérome, Paolo Veronese, Carlo Crivelli, are only a few of the artists who have recorded the multifarious colours and faces of this land and its people, and then recreated them on canvas.

What is special about some of these painters is that their works have led to the creation of other works of art in literature. Lear is prominent among the painters who dealt with Albanian subjects. Two of his Albanian landscapes, "Endless Acroceraunian Mountains" and "Horse of Tomor", are known to have inspired the English poet Alfred Tennyson write a few verses on the Albanian landscape:

Tomohri, Athos, all things fair
With such a pencil, such a pen,
You shadow forth to distant men...
I read and felt that I was there! (qtd in Hudhri 121)

Similarly, Léon Gérome's paintings of Albania have inspired poets Théophile Gautier and José Maria de Hérédia to write about this country and its people even without being there in person. The country possesses a rich literary legacy, among which, a wealth of oral literature, epic poetry and other various narrative traditions. The foreign writings which deal with the Albanian theme are earlier than the first book in Albanian, *Meshari* (1555). According to literary critic Refik Kadija, such writings go back to antiquity where Illyria and Illyrians were mentioned not only in the historical works of Pliny and Plutarch, but also in the literary works of Plautus, Ovid, Virgil, Horace, and even Aeschylus. (248)

A large body of travel literature exists on Albania (given the small area of the country) and its people, especially produced by 19th century travellers. Prominent among them is the work of Edith Durham. But well-known figures of world literature have also taken an interest in Albanian matters. Outstanding among them is the British poet George Byron (1788-1824) who is credited with opening up Albania to the English readers with his *Childe Harold's Pilgrimage* (1812):

Land of Albania! Where Iskander rose,
Theme of the young, and beacon of the wise,
And he his namesake, whose oft-baffled foes
Shrunk from his deeds of chivalrous emprize;
Land of Albania! let me bend mine eyes
Oh thee, thou rugged Nurse of savage men!
The Cross descends, thy Minarets arise,
And the pale Crescent sparkles in the glen,
Through many cypress-grove within each city's ken
...(Canto II, Stanza 38)

Byron's Albanian theme is also known to have influenced his contemporary writer P.B. Shelley who dedicated 16 lines to the figure of Ali Pasha in his *Hellas* (1822). In addition, Byron's description of Albania is known to have inspired another equally well known of his contemporaries, politician and writer Benjamin Disraeli, who set off for Albania in 1830 following Byron's tracks. He delighted in the landscape of Ioannina at the foot of "purple mountains of picturesque form" (Elsie 8) and Ali Pasha's palace which he described in his *Contarini Fleming*. Albania was also the inspiration for his novel *The Rise of Iskander*.

In the English literature prior to Byron, there can be found an indirect reference to Albania by William Shakespeare through the mention of Illyria (the old name of present-day Albania) in the *Twelfth Night* (1623). In his *Comedy of Errors* (*As you like it*), the Albanian city of Durr's has been mentioned seven times under its Roman name 'Epidamnum', also accompanied with notes explaining its meaning at least in one of the work's editions. (Kadija 252)

Literary tourism in Albania might not be an industry *per se* but there must certainly be people (including senior citizens) sufficiently interested in the works of various writers, most importantly three time Nobel Prize nominee and Booker prize winner Ismail Kadare whose birthplace Gjirokastra (also hometown of the infamous dictator Enver Hoxha) and house turned into a museum, have much to offer.

Other tourists to follow the footsteps of Byron who "[a]dventured on a shore unknown/ Which all admire, but many dread to view [...]/ Lands scarce noticed in historic tales. ("CHP" 2.43.4; 2.46.3-4) Currently, there is a privately-run Byron trail in Albania. Tourists' curiosity about Byron in Albania is typically divided between admiration for the man (he is well known for his eccentric personality) and his work. Another group of tourists seems to follow the trail from some deeper interest and engagement. This is the case of former British ambassador in Albania, Fiona Mclleham who states, "Feels as if I was living in ancient Scotland." (Serjani, my translation)

In addition, for several tourists, this particular literary tour seems to have included more elements (historic, cultural, natural) as it did for Dutch writer Tessa de Loo:

[...] you drew me ... into an Oriental world whose existence I had not suspected when I stood on the Pantokrator pondering the nature of the land beyond the grey mountains. I became enchanted by the exotic décor, the mishmash of peoples in their colourful costumes, the Pasha who could so

easily show cruelty at one moment and tenderness the next ... Life in a staid street in Holland at the end of the 20th century could not compete with that. I wanted only one thing: to go with you. I wanted to visit Ali Pasha too, as a spectre from a future age, as a voyeur, as a nostalgia sufferer. (De Loo 2)
[...]

Like Tessa, future tourists might want to learn more not just about the poet, but also about the 'uncommon' country he chose to visit:

When I read that letter, my old love for Byron came flooding back. I decided to travel with him, on horseback, making the same journey—even if it was two centuries later. I wanted to get to know not just Byron but Albania too... Contrasted to this all, life in a cold Dutch street had to end. I only wanted one thing: come with you. I would even go to Ali Pasha, as a shadow from the future, a traveller, a nostalgic ...
Once, I had stood on the top of the Pantokrator on Corfu and looked to the east, intrigued by the massive grey hulks of the mountains on the other side of the narrow strait. They looked like the backs of patiently waiting elephants; if you reached out your hand far enough you could touch them. Only to pull it back again quickly because what you did was forbidden. (1-2)

Louella and Robin Hanbury Tenison visited Albania in 2007 following the Byron trail when they were in their late sixties and early seventies respectively. ... For them, in addition to its literary motives, the journey turned out to be a wonderful one *per se* thanks to the wonderful natural landscapes it offered: "In this pristine wilderness of mature forests and deep valleys, wildlife thrives. ... The silence was absolute ... and the uninterrupted forest that spread in all directions was truly stupendous." (Tenison 160)

They gathered prior knowledge before setting off for their journey:

As I began researching Albania I became increasingly excited. I discovered that it is one of the wildest and most unspoilt places in Europe and that it has a rich and fascinating history as well as some of the greatest military

and literary links with Britain. (Tenison xx) As I dug deeper and deeper into anything Albanian, it was the literary connections that interested me most. Shakespeare set *Twelfth Night* in Illyria. (Tenison xxiv) ...
I was hooked and began making plans to ride in the footsteps of these past travellers, artists, kings, poets, sportsmen and idealists. I wanted to see a side of Albania few foreigners had seen for many years ... A whole new world of history, romance, adventure and wild landscapes was luring me to a country which I was beginning to realise deserved to be much better known. Albania! (Tenison 24)

If Tenison had not done some private research, he might have never learned about and gotten the drive to travel to Albania! Unfortunately, there is little recognition of literature as a tourist resource by the Albanian tourist authorities and little is made of it in terms of promotion.

However, prospective senior tourists might enjoy following the Byron trail whose being a relatively unbeaten track makes it pretty challenging. This is actually one of the strong points of this trail, in spite of the several difficulties:

When night fell, they would read Lord Byron's poetry and excerpts from the diary of his friend, John Cam Hobhouse. When the sun rose, they would jump on their horses and ride the paths the British poet took in 1809 in southern Albania. (Hoxha)

We saw a side of Albania few are privileged to see and it touched us. We were lucky to do so before whatever changes lie ahead come to pass. (Tenison 193)

The beauty of this magnificent wild countryside now came into sharp focus, as, looking down onto the valleys, one could almost picture Byron, Hobhouse and company trekking slowly and laboriously, through the dense woodlands below (Gregory)

The impressions tourists left online or published in book form might be used by the Albanian tourism authorities to organize, advertise and better promote the literary aspect of the country for prospective senior tourists.

Conclusion

This paper has tackled two issues: extending the range of countries involved in the senior sector (Albania was presented as an option) and including literary tourism as part of the travel packages designed for the elderly.

Research shows that travel is a key priority for senior citizens. Albania is suggested as a destination for the interesting and less well known historic and cultural values it has. The paper also suggested that the Albanian authorities should actively promote the country as well as develop special tourism policies and facilities for this group.

Senior citizens contribute to the European off-season tourism, stimulating economic growth and jobs, which is why literary tourism should be encouraged as an option. If well planned and promoted it could bring an interesting turn to the senior travel industry as well as to the economy.

Works Cited

Bardhyli, Alda. "Një franceze në gjurmët e Bajronit." *Gazeta Shqip*. 17 Oct. 2006. Web. 20 September 2011.

Barke, Michael. "'Inside' and 'Outside' Writings on Spain." *Literature and Tourism: essays in the reading and writing of tourism*. Eds. Robinson, Mike and Hans Christian Andersen. London: Thomson, 2003. 80-104. Print.

Blacksearoamer. "Ioannina to Tepelena." 17 Nov. 2012. Web. 20 Nov, 2012.

Byron, Gordon. *Childe Harold's Pilgrimage.* Oxford: Clarendon Press, 1980. Print.

De Loo, Tessa. *In Byron's Footsteps.* Trans. A. Brown. London: Armchair Traveller, 2010. Print.

Dublin UNESCO City of Literature. October 2009. Web. 5 January 2015.

Elder Treks. Web. 20 November 2014.

Elsie, Robert. *Albanian Literature: A Short History.* London: Palgrave, 2005. Print.

Gregory, Allen. Albanian Byron Conference. 2009. Web. 14 December 2011.

Herbert, David. "Literary places, tourism and the heritage experience." *Annals of Tourism Research.* 28.2 (2001). 312-33. Print.

Hoxha, Rudina. "In the footsteps of Lord Byron 202 years later." *Southeast Europe.* 7 Sep. 2011. Web. 20 April 2013.

Hudhri, Ferid. *Shqipëria dhe shqiptarët në vepra të piktorëve të huaj.* Tiranë: Shtëpia botuese 8 Nëntori, 1990.

Kadija, Refik. "Tema dhe motive shqiptare në letërsinë angleze të traditës." *Studime Shqiptare* 12. Shkodër: Camaj-Pipa, 2003.

Maltby, Deborah. "The Redemptive Myth of the Rural: Thomas Hardy's Literary Tourists and Englishness." Literary Tourism and Nineteenth-Century Culture. Institute of English Studies. 7 Nov. 2007 Web. 21 January 2009.

Patterson, Ian R. *Growing Older: Tourism and Leisure Behaviour of Older Adults.* Wallingford, Oxfordshire, UK: CABI Pub, 2006. Print.

Pearson, Michael. *Imagined Places: Journeys into Literary America.* New York: Syracuse University Press, 1992. Print.

Prajag, Girish "Senior Travelers' Motivations and Future Behavioral Intentions: The Case Of Nice." *Journal of Travel & Tourism Marketing.* 29 (2012): 665-81. Web. 22 December 2014.

Robinson, Mike and Hans Christian Andersen, eds. *Literature and Tourism: essays in the reading and writing of tourism.* London: Thomson, 2003. Print.

Serjani, Engjëll. "Dy ambasadore në kërkim të Lord Bajronit." *Gazeta Shqip*. 1 December 2010. Web. 8 March 2013.

Sutherland, John. "Great books I've walked." *The Guardian*. 20 May 2006. Web 30 March 2009.

Tenison, Robin H. *Land of Eagles: Riding through Europe's Forgotten Country*. London: I.B. Tauris, 2009. Print.

"Tourism for Seniors." European Commission. Web. 17 November 2014.

Watson, Nicola. *The Literary Tourist*. Houndmills: Palgrave, 2006. Print.

"Almost Fatally Disoriented"
Tourism and Aging in Moritz Thomsen's
The Saddest Pleasure

Simone Francescato

> It struck me that we must have the most geriatric tourists in the world; and, even though they were treated like kindergarteners, they were curious about the world. For them, bless their yellow pants and blue shoes, travel was part of growing old.
>
> (PAUL THEROUX, The Old Patagonian Express 247)

An unusual representation of elderly tourism is at the center of a rather forgotten masterpiece of contemporary American travel writing, Moritz Thomsen's *The Saddest Pleasure: A Journey on Two Rivers* (1990). Paul Theroux, a longtime friend and admirer of the author, found in this book "not just a report of a journey, but a memoir, an autobiography, a confession, a foray into South American topography and history, a travel narrative, with observations of books, music, and life in general; in short, what the best travel books are" ("The Exile Moritz Thomsen" 425). In *The Cambridge Companion to American Travel Writing*, Terry Caesar even came to define it as "quite possibly the finest American travel book of all—the most politically sophisticated, the most emotionally rich" ("South of the Border" 190). Virtually neglected by critics, Moritz Thomsen (1915-1991) has always been an outcast for the literary establishment, a fact most likely due to his voluntary confinement to an isolated corner of the

Third World. The rebel son of a tyrannical man—a multi-millionaire capitalist—from the Pacific Northwest, Thomsen participated in several bombing missions during World War Two, which deeply shocked him and left indelible traces in his memory. In his forties he joined the Peace Corps in Ecuador, an experience he recounted in his first and, perhaps, most remembered memoir, *Living Poor: A Peace Corps Chronicle* (1969). At the end of the 1960s he made up his mind to settle permanently in Ecuador, in the small town of Rio Verde, where he stayed until the end of his life. There he lived in solitude as a poor man among the poorest, helping, not without frequent altercations and misunderstandings, a local black worker to establish and run his own farm. Meanwhile, he published two more memoirs, *The Farm on the River of Emeralds* (1978), centered on his life in Rio Verde, and *The Saddest Pleasure* (1990), which focused on a leisure trip to Brazil in the late Seventies.[1] This latter book, which can be considered as the last part of the 'trilogy' begun with *Living Poor*, explores with extraordinary depth late-life traveling, and its complex relationship with memory and identity.

My reading of this work resonates with Amelia De Falco's recent theorization of the analogies between narrating and aging, tracing them to a representational travel context. Both being manifestations of human nature, narrating and aging are central to the formation as well as to the disruption of one's identity over time. If identity is essentially a self-narration which leads to a rather stable interpretation of subjectivity, aging into old age, as De Falco has it, implies a progressive alteration of such interpretation, which ultimately "[dissolves the] facades of wholeness and stability that obscure the fundamentally unstable human condition" (126). Thomsen's book, in particular, explores the effect of this process on the *traveling subject*, depicting how mobility leads him to question previously acquired interpretations of himself and/in the world.

---

1 | For a short biographical account of Thomsen's life, see Lowry.

Displacing the Leisure Traveler

The Saddest Pleasure vividly shows the links among narrating, aging, and traveling—and the concomitant disruption/redefinition of identity—by staging a double movement in time and space, mainly identified by the *two* rivers referred to in the subtitle: the Amazon river, which stands for Thomsen's present time, and the Esmeraldas River in North-Eastern Ecuador, which represents his recent past. More precisely, the book interweaves (at least) four temporally and spatially different memoir narratives: Thomsen's present travels in Brazil, his more recent past in Rio Verde, his early life back in the US, and his experience as a bombardier in Europe during WWII. Such interweaving can be seen in association with his identity crisis prompted by the fact that this tourist trip is largely forced on Thomsen by outer circumstances: indeed, his partner Ramon asks him to stop working in the farm and retire, disappointed by his scarce productivity, but also worried about his poor health.

In the book, Thomsen emerges as a prosaic version of the epic heroes of classical age travels,[2] standing out as some sort of postmodern Ulysses who embarks on a late-life rite of passage, whose aims, though, are unclear and indefinite. The first chapter, "Despedida", derives its emotional grip from the aching description of Thomsen parting with Ramon and his family, especially the children Moncho and Martita. Obliquely presented in the guise of a detached observation of the melodramatic way of saying farewell in Latin America, this chapter, by contrast, powerfully stages the existential anguish of an expatriate who has no family ties and has cut off any association with his former life in the US. In doing so, it also sheds an ironic light on concepts such as "leisure travel" and "retirement,"[3] which

---

2 | See Leed 7.

3 | The concept of retirement has been described as intrinsically ambivalent. Joel S. Shavishinsky, for instance, observes that: "In the United States today retirement is the last of life's major active phases, and perhaps the most mystifying to those who have yet to reach it. The hopes and fears it

belong to a prototypically Western and capitalist vision of society, one which also excludes the elderly from active life: "How awful it was to be of no use to anyone, to awaken in the mornings and be unable to think of a single reason for crawling out of bed. One day out of desperation it occurred to me that finally I might make a trip./ I arranged everything in near secrecy—tickets, visa, traveler's checks. The trip was a symbol of rejection, humiliation, and uselessness" (3-4).

Thomsen's involvement in a post-retirement leisure trip—an obvious pursuit for any other American citizen of his age—alienates him from the radical lifestyle he has led up to that point in Rio Verde and re-positions him, at least momentarily, within a typically Western ageist discourse. He feels so disoriented that he has the impression of vanishing amid numbers and statistics ("I am sixty-three years old now, have been very sick, and I see myself as a statistic that proves that old men forced into retirement are especially vulnerable to death's kiss", 9). Above all, Thomsen's trip leads him to elaborate on his ongoing romantic plan to take part in the life of poor people (which he compares to a "hopelessly romantic symphony", 3), making him realize that in all these years he had never felt the need to take a trip because he always felt as though he were a "tourist in [his] own house" (3). No longer part of his 'substitute family' in Rio Verde (Ramon's family), he is now afraid of the possibility of dying in a decidedly anonymous and unheroic way ("a superfluous old man", 29), instead of "[dropping] in the sun with a machete in [his] hand [...] as a kind of triumph"(3) like any other local worker would. What Thomsen feels is a sense of generalized displacement and unbeara-

---

invites are both fundamental and contradictory. It evokes ideas of freedom and frailty, loss and opportunity, and a sense of time that is either pregnant with possibility or else weighs heavily on the soul. For some, retirement is the promise to fulfill dreams deferred, for others the face of dread. Some people expect from it new forms of life, liberty, and the pursuit of happiness where others envision a failed landscape populated by the workless and worthless" (4).

ble self-exposure ("This trip, which has scarcely begun, has already changed me [...] not only do I see things in cleaner, truer colors, but certain aspects of my character have become magnified to an alarming degree. I have become a stranger to myself [...] I detect vast new capacities for impatience, resentful anger, and cynicism", 17).

Terribly missing a home he could never call his own, he realizes that he is now unable to reconnect with the modern world around him, which makes its lurking reappearance in the fancy-dressed "rich men's whores" at the duty-free shops at Bogotá airport. Thomsen's expectations are almost immediately disappointed and very early on during his trips he falls victim to disenchantment:

> What I had expected was a journey into romanticism, into the slower, timeless world of the near past; perhaps even so far as a childhood, which one, perhaps falsely, remembers as a place of purity, strong colors, excruciating authenticities./What I know now in a sudden rush is that that old world has gone; things have changed way past my capacity to understand or accept. I am like some Rip Van Winkle who has awakened and wandered into a present that fills him with confusion and despair. (20)

The analogy with Washington Irving's "Rip Van Winkle", a classic story Thomas J. Cole described as an early protest against the advance of modern market society (*and* the concurring devaluation of aging people in American history)[4] perfectly conveys Thomsen's shocking returning to 'civilization' and its most depreciatory aspects. Thomsen finds himself associating this trip with those he made with his wealthy family forty years earlier (9), remembering that, already at a tender age, he saw Western tourists traveling to the

---

4 | According to Cole, "Rip Van Winkle" (1819) would represent "an ironic protest against 'the civilizing process'—the continuing rationalization of individual behavior in a market society [...] Rip's fate foreshadows the obsolescence of the old man in a secular society where women become rulers of the home, productivity becomes the primary criterion of a man's worth, and patriarchy becomes a maudlin compensation for powerlessness" (75).

poorest parts of the planet "as unnecessary to the suffering world as some mysteriously moving cancer." (9-11) He seems to realize the contiguity between the violent early European colonization of South America in the past and the economic exploitation perpetrated in the present by rich countries like the United States, as epitomized in the considerable affluence of wealthy foreign tourists.[5]

In spite of the uneasiness with which he acts out his role of leisure traveler, Thomsen initially approaches Brazil with an expectation of exoticness that is typically touristy. Believing that what he is about to visit is a largely wild and unexplored world, he somehow enacts a teenage-like dream of escape from the repressive rules of his native culture. While flying on the plane over the Amazon forest to Rio, for instance, he imagines this space as "an immense, oceanic land, the world's last mysterious and only half-tamed area" (24), remembering how it powerfully excited his youthful fancy:

Now once more I begin to see this invisible land below me as I had imagined it many years ago. At thirteen, bursting with the lusts of puberty, my sexual fantasies had transported me to South America [...] When my sexual meditations were involved with the Brazilian jungles, having little fuel to fire my erotic imaginings, I often put myself in a circle around a campfire with a hundred naked Indians. [...] Until my sophomore year in high school words like Brazil and Amazonia had been powerful aphrodisiacs; even now they held a certain exciting power. [...] Around us are the mourning ghosts of Bates and Wallace, who worked furiously but left unidentified another fifty thousand species of bugs and plants. And isn't there another ghost out there, a kid in khaki shorts and tennis shoes who peeks through the slats of palm fronds at humping bodies and manipulates himself to the rhythm of jungle bongos? (26-27)

---

5 | Thomsen associates his despotic father, a capitalist and privileged tourist, with ruthless conquerors of the past like Pizarro and Cortez (see 71-72).

As soon as Thomsen sets foot on land and starts to get acquainted with Brazil, however, this exoticized picture crumbles, leaving him trapped in what he defines as a "post-coitus triste", where the possibility of unproblematic enjoyment is out of question, and 'reality' looms more starkly than ever. In his first glimpse during a short flight connection in Manaus, he has some sort of insight and observes: "Christ, I had got it all wrong. This air is all warm and sensuous innocence. As it rushes over me, instantly I am educated to the foolishness of having for a lifetime associated this land with my youthful erections" (27).[6]

THE FRUSTRATED EXPATRIATE AND THE INDOMITABLE TOURISTS

Thomsen's failure to accomplish a satisfying tourist agenda has a highly subversive effect in this memoir as it violates the "ethics of pleasure" underlying the very notion of leisure travel,[7] and, by contrast, gives rise to a painful self-searching tension. Seldom enjoyable or relaxing, Thomsen's trip often resembles an effort to survive ("I am not making a trip now as much as simply trying to stay alive, 102), where he drifts in search of some kind of deeper existential meaning and tries to put together those portions of his identity he had kept apart during his long years abroad: it is significant, in this

---

6 | The exoticness and sensuality of the Southern hemisphere is also linked to his grandfather's secret marriage to a Mexican woman, which his grandson experiences as a 'revitalizing' flaw in the apparently perfect life of his wealthy upper class family.

7 | For the relationship between tourism and the "commandment to enjoy" in capitalist society, see MacCannell, 52-53. The ambivalence of this trip allows this memoir to elude the two clichés of contemporary travel writing, which according to Holland and Huggan, consist in "the hypertheorization of travel-as-displacement" and "the naively untheorized celebration of travel-as-freedom" (IX).

regard, that when Thomsen lies ill in bed for almost a week in Salvador de Bahia, he spends his time reading Conrad's *Heart of Darkness*, a book which gives voice to the appalling fragmentation of the white man's ego in an unknown universe ("then I go back to bed and lie there coughing, sad and passive, with Conrad stretching his open pages across my chest." 102).

Thomsen's self-searching tension begins in a central scene of the text, where he observes his naked body in front of a six-foot mirror in a hotel room in Rio:

It has been a long time since I have studied myself so carefully and with such horror. It is all there, the things I had suspected but not thought much about—the sagging stomach, my ass flabby with grossness, my shriveled sex, a timid rosebud peeking out through tired public hair. How cruel my mouth looks with most of my teeth sitting over there in a glass of water. It has been a year since I left there where I didn't even own a mirror; in Quito under a dim light I could make out that face that needed shaving; I am looking at myself for almost the first time in ten years, and can see at last that I had been truly broken by that time in the jungle and that old age, when it came, came as swiftly as a street bully who with blows and blunt instruments shatters a man in a moment. This is what Ramón had seen when he told me that I must leave the farm. Well, well, no wonder. I have been betrayed by my gross body, *this aging stranger* who lies staring at me so resentfully and which in no way is a reflection of how I see myself. "There he is, *your double*; why can't you be friends with him?" It is an idea instantly repudiated. (emphasis added, 44)

I read this passage as an exemplification of the uncanniness experienced by a man facing the very fact of aging. Following De Falco—who expanded the theory of the mirror stage of aging originally formulated by Kathleen Woodward[8]—I here describe the *uncanny*

---

8 | In *Aging and Its Discontents* (1991) Kathleen Woodward postulates the existence of a "mirror stage of old age", which would represent a variation on Lacan's mirror stage of infancy (Ecrits 1966). In this stage, the old

as the disavowal, denial, and acknowledgment of one's self brought about by the realization of the disjunction of one's altered image (the aging body) and one's perceived inner consistency (10). Likewise, in this scene Thomsen's shocked reaction to the vision of his aged body ("this aging stranger [...] your double") reveals the gap between an unexpected bodily narration appallingly displaying the passing of time and an idealized and stubbornly preserved self-narration. Thomsen also recalls, quite to the point, that he never owned a mirror after relocating to Quito—that is after being rejected from the farm as some sort of useless tool—and we can interpret this as an unconscious act to preserve an idealized image of himself as young, healthy and capable of continuing his radical lifestyle.

Thomsen's experience of uncanniness in the book is not entirely demoralizing, as it is paralleled by a considerable expansion of his creativity ("Something about making a trip has triggered my imagination and I find myself inventing the lives of perfect strangers, giving them jobs, problems, passions", 12). The contradictions he embodies (he is white and rich, but leads the life of a poor man; he's embarked on a leisurely trip, but he's not a tourist proper) lead him to speculate on both his self-protective attitude of identifying with the locals (an identification impossible to achieve) as well as on his relation to other American tourists he meets on his way.

His speculations are strongly rendered in the chapter dedicated to Recife-Natal-Fortaleza, which precedes the account of Thomsen's first contact with the Amazon river. This is the part of the memoir where Thomsen most passionately expresses his love for South American people (describing them as "a super-race that strives to triumph over the awfulness of life by the purity of its perceptions, its openness to experience, and its freedom from guilt", 131) and at

---

persons who look at themselves in the mirror do not see an integrated self reflected, but feel alienated from the image of their aged body, which they believe has somehow betrayed them.

the same time engages in the closest examination of other fellow tourists.⁹

In this chapter, his determination to mingle with the locals is so strong as to produce a shift in the narrating voice from the first person singular to the first person plural. This is evident, for instance, in a passage where he imagines joining some locals who are anxiously watching a football match in a bar, hoping for the victory of their national team ("And *we* need to win", emphasis added), noticing a little later how victory, unfortunately unattained, stood out for them, and for himself too, as a compensation for their poverty and insignificance in the eyes of the world ("Now that *we* have lost, it begins to seem that losing had always been inevitable, only one more thing that is lost and that is going to be lost", 140-1, emphasis added).¹⁰ This kind of 'imagined identification' can be interpreted by resorting to Terry Caesar's words, as he observes that in this book "an American suffers the identity of another continent in order to come to terms with his own history not only as an individual but also as a representative American" (*Forgiving the Boundaries* 150-2).

Thomsen, however, does not seek redemption by entirely distancing himself from his country and his countrymen, rather preferring to observe them through some sort of ironic participation. Later on in the same chapter, sure enough, as he finds himself observing a group of "incredibly old American tourists," his narration abandons the conventions of the memoir, curiously veering towards the visionary,¹¹ as if to more powerfully convey his impressions of

---

9 | See how in the book Thomsen often rejects the information provided by guidebooks, whose only scope is to make the tourist feel at ease, rather than help him understand what he sees around him. See 138-139.

10 | Such identification is also explored by Caesar (*Forgiving the Boundaries* 152).

11 | Much like Paul Theroux did in his travel book *The Old Patagonian Express* (see in particular Chapter X, "The Atlantic Railway: The 12:00 to Limón"), here Thomsen employs some fellow American tourist as a counterpart to himself, and his critique is tempered by partial identification. This

other fellow elderly American travelers and their existential plight. The passage is worth quoting in full:

Though they display the stigmata, though they are archetypes, they are far past that age when one might be tempted to hold them up to ridicule as American tourists. Their extreme deterioration is humbling. In the way they huddle together, in the uncertain way they talk to the waiter, half-arrogant, half-apologetic, in the way they look around them, timid and blinking, what is most evident is that they are frightened and confused. They are almost fatally disoriented. Yes indeed, here, if I am not, is the living proof: travel is the saddest of the pleasures.

They are thousands of miles, separated from anything familiar [...] Everything is strange, every minute is filled with a rushing strangeness, a vague menace, a jabbing reminder of estrangement, a hint of their own complete irrelevance. But behind their terror, for this strangeness and irrelevance cannot but constantly remind them of their age and their vulnerability to age's last demand, they are displaying a magnificent courage. These four are part of the real aristocracy of the aged; most of their friends who still live are rocking in the semiprivate rooms of rest homes. These four refuse to give in to their weariness; they will keep going until they drop. They have come to see new things in the world, and if the things they have seen are not exactly what they were promised by the travel agent or don't seem to have much connection with what they had imagined, they will conceal their disillusion, their awakening awareness of a banal world, and a general unfocused horror. [...]

---

is how he introduces the passage: "But let me shift my characters around a bit and juxtapose the other four Americans that I saw in another place not far from here; [...] Instead of an airport restaurant where they more properly belong, let me put them in this bus station where they sit drinking orange juice and fearfully toying with plates of scrambled eggs", 144). Thomsen himself later explains the reason behind this narrative license, stating: "This is not the first time I have moved my characters around and put them beside someone else who will, perhaps, better Iluminate their qualities or my feelings about them" (146).

> Without wanting to, no, without even asking themselves if they want it or not, they will insist upon seeing everything that has been promised them in the tourist handouts. They are as ready, as unthinking as combat soldiers who storm some barricade.
> What confounds them and turns the trip into a kind of dream so ephemeral and fading that it cannot be discussed is the identical nature of the hotels where they have stayed [...] And of course they are protected. They will be protected by these cement hotels with the roof-top restaurants, the wall-to-wall carpeting, and the arctic chill of the air conditioning from whatever is real in South America (144-145)

Here Thomsen provides an incredibly acute psychological portrait of a few elderly tourists, prototypically American, whom he believes to be privileged ones ("aristocrats of the ages") among their untraveled peers, as, for them, this journey largely represents the last chance at finally overcoming the boundaries of a former physical and mental national 'confinement'. Pointing out their profound disorientation, he ironically praises their "magnificent courage," their determination to finally live up to their dreams of seeing "new things in the world," only to highlight their self-centeredness ("they will insist upon seeing everything that has been promised them") and hypocritical curiosity ("they will conceal their disillusion"), in compliance with a tourist industry that keeps them inside a bubble, preventing them from having any contact with a reality that lurks only momentarily in the guise of a "general unfocused horror". He subtly correlates these tourists with "unthinking combat soldiers", hinting at their unaware involvement in their country's imperialist and economic exploitation of Latin America.

Conclusion

According to Caesar once more, "Thomsen appears in this book as one of those rare Americans who did not return home, because he represents himself as one of the world's homeless, who has to invent a space for himself day-by-day, while nations act out their follies at a vast distance from the millions of individual lives so arbitrarily comprehended within their respective borders" (*Forgiving the Boundaries*, 156). In Caesar's view, it is Thomsen's self-imposed homelessness that affords him a special perspective on the relationship between the North and the South of the American continent in *The Saddest Pleasure*. In my reading, however, such perspective is significantly enriched and complicated by Thomsen's reflections on his role as a reluctant tourist and his ironic participation with the experience of other elderly tourist compatriots, also signaled by the reprise of a line from the aforementioned passage as the title of the whole book ("travel is the saddest of the pleasures"). Thomsen projects upon those tourists, and articulates through them, the sense of existential meaninglessness of his life as an aging expatriate after his forced retirement. As one who, perhaps too late in life, desperately ached to be part of the less fortunate and now finds himself reduced to an ironic caricature of a Western elderly tourist, he cannot help but find some depressing identification with those who never had, and never will have, the chance to see the squalor, but also the beauty, of real life in the Southern hemisphere of America.[12]

---

12 | The final part of this memoir is set on a ship navigating the labyrinthine canals of the Amazon, a setting which perfectly resonates with Thomsen's increasing disorientation ("Now that I was getting old I had a horror of becoming superfluous", 238). In the midst of complex socio-political, philosophical, and existential reflections on the destiny of a planet tortured by humanity with all its greed, corruption, and hopelessness, Thomsen seems to recover at least some confidence in art and in his identity as a writer, thanks to the soothing beauty of the music played by a Brazilian duo aboard the ship. But there is little reconciliation in the end, as readers are left with two characters embodying contrasting stances: a Brazilian poet from Manaus who holds that the destruction of the planet is inevitable, but will finally bring a positive change in man, and Hecrik, a Dutch theologian and nihilist, who thinks that man cannot change because God gave him the mis-

The originality of Thomsen's memoir, to conclude, is not only to be found in the author's exceptional proximity to the material he treats, but also in the way in which this book plays with the figure of the tourist, exposing the implications and contradictions of leisure (late-life) travel in our contemporary age.

WORKS CITED

Caesar, Terry. *Forgiving the Boundaries. Home as Abroad in American Travel Writing*. Athens GE: The University of Georgia Press, 1995. Print.

—. "South of the Border: American Travel Writing in Latin America." *The Cambridge Companion to American Travel Writing*. Ed. Alfred Bendixen and Judith Hamera, Cambridge UK: Cambridge University Press, 2009. 180-96. Print.

Cole, Thomas J. *The Journey of Life: A Cultural History of Aging in America*. Cambridge MA: Cambridge University Press, 1992. Print.

DeFalco, Amelia, *Uncanny Subjects: Aging in Contemporary Narrative*, Columbus: Ohio State University Press, 2010. Print.

Holland, Patrick and Graham Huggan, eds. *Tourists with Typewriters: Critical Reflections onC ontemporary Travel Writing*. Ann Arbor: The University of Michigan Press, 1998. Print.

Leed, Eric J. *The Mind of the Traveler: From Gilgamesh to Global Tourism*. New York: Basic Books, 1992. Print.

Lowry, Mark. "The Last Days of Moritz Thomsen." *South American Explorer*, 51 (Spring 1998): 12-20.

MacCannell, Dean. *The Ethics of Sightseeing*. Berkeley and Los Angeles: University of California Press, 2011. Print.

Shavishinsky, Joel S. *Breaking the Watch: The Meanings of Retirement in America*. Ithaca NY: Cornell University Press, 2000. Print.

---

sion to destroy his creation—a bleak and misanthropic image which brings the book to its close.

Theroux, Paul. "The Exile Moritz Thomsen." *Fresh Air Fiend: Travel Writings 1985-2000*. New York: Vintage, 2000. 425-30. Print.

Theroux, Paul. *The Old Patagonian Express. By Train Through the Americas*. London: Penguin, 2008. Print.

Thomsen, Moritz. *The Farm on the River of Emeralds*. New York: Vintage, 1989. Print.

—. *Living Poor: A Peace Corps Chronicle*. University of Washington Press, 1990. Print.

—. *The Saddest Pleasure: A Journey on Two Rivers*, London: The Sumach Press, 1991. Print.

Woodward, Kathleen. *Aging and Its Discontents: Freud and Other Fictions*. Bloomington: Indiana University Press, 1991.

"A Man Should Be Able to Take a Trip if He Wants"

Senior Tourism in Oscar Casares' *Amigoland*

Ulla Kriebernegg

> Acquiring mobility is often analogous to a struggle for acquiring new subjectivity.
> (UTENG AND CRESSWELL 2)

> Contemporary depictions of elderly characters on the road again do more than expand literary and film road genres; they reconfigure expectations of old age in a way that stands to make elderly mobility important enough to matter socially.
> (CHIVERS 214)

This essay deals with a very specific kind of senior tourism—that of seniors who escape the specter of long-term residential care in order to embark on journeys that prove life-altering. I will investigate senior tourism as a major site of cultural identity formation, memory, and cultural heritage by proving some general observations on care home escape stories, and then discussing how mobility, space, and place inform an old man's identity construction in Oscar Casares' first novel *Amigoland* (2009). "A man should be able to take a trip if he wants"— these are the words Don Fidencio, the novel's protagonist, states (205) before walking out of the nursing home. For a couple of days, he becomes a "senior tourist," traveling together with his younger brother Don Celestino and his brother's lover Socorro almost three hundred miles in a taxi from Brownsville, Texas, across the US-Mexican border to the city of Linares. He sleeps in hotels, eats in restaurants, and enjoys the street life in Matamoros and other places along the way. Contrary to his two fellow travelers' expectations, however, he does not join them on their return trip, but decides to spend the remainder of his days at El Rancho de La Paz in Mexico, an "idyllic chronotope" of family life, to use Mikhail Bakhtin's words (226). In the novel the third person narration offers all three travelers' perspectives on the journey to Mexico as focalization oscillates between the three main characters.

When protagonists in "nursing home escape narratives"[1] flee institutional confinement, they not only transgress spatial boundaries, encounter and overcome obstacles, and perform acts of spatial resistance, but also change their social position: they leave their roles as care home patients or residents (sometimes even prisoners) behind to become senior tourists. The motives for characters to leave their homes differ in each escape story and are not always grounded first and foremost in the unbearable world of a care home often modeled in literature and film after what Erving Goffman calls a "total institution" (14). *Amigoland*, as most "care home escape novels" a generic cross-over combining elements of the road novel and the prison escape story, presents one of the main reasons why fictional characters run away from institutional confinement: the quest for individual identity in late life. The home, as is also the case in *Amigoland*, can be read as a metaphor for the protagonist's discontent with the static confinement so frequently ascribed to old age. By means of contrast to the open road, the home reinforces the representation of the protagonist's wish for self-determination and agency. *Amigo-*

---

1 | The "escape narrative" seems to be an emerging sub-genre of the care home novel. This article is part of my larger research project on the care home novel as an emerging genre, *Putting Age in its Place: Intersections of Age and Space in Contemporary North American Care Home Narratives* (in preparation with Winter, Heidelberg).

land portrays an old man's resistance against homogenization and marginalization in institutional care as a powerful expression of his wish for social participation. In addition to such "push-factors," "pull factors" also play an important role: Don Fidencio needs to return to the place of his grandfather's childhood in Mexico to fulfil a promise he had made to his "Papá Grande." His trip to Mexico enables him to find out about the mysterious story of his grandfather's kidnapping by Indians that had become a contested family myth. The voyage is a dual journey, a journey of the mind and of the body, leading to a reevaluation of his identity and his relationship to his brothers.

As many of the protagonists in care home escape novels, Don Fidencio is struggling, as Uteng and Cresswell put it (2), to acquire a new kind of subjectivity by changing his position. The newly emerging genre of care home escape stories centers on the spiritual and physical journeys aged protagonists take and which change them forever, challenging the myth of old age as static and immobile. "Lack of movement is characteristic of decrepit age," Kathleen Woodward contends: "If movement bespeaks life, immobility—lack of movement—is akin to death, and inertia verges dangerously on the inert" ("Instant" 53). Escape narratives and journeys counteract the myth of immobility in old age and celebrate the protagonists' resistance to the inertia forced upon them by institutional life.

Thomas R. Cole analyzes the topos of life as a journey in his groundbreaking book *The Journey of Life* (1992), tracing it back to biblical traditions and "The Aging Pilgrim's Progress in the New World," as chapter two is entitled (32-47). "The journey is among the most pervasive themes in world literature. Folk tales, poetry, drama, fiction, art, and religious teaching are filled with male heroes who set out from safe but constricting origins, undergo a series of adventures that transform them, and eventually reach or fail to reach a goal, or prize, or spiritual home," Cole states (xxxii). The journey narrative which is usually a quest narrative is traditionally associated with a young man's experience of (self)discovery and liberation from social constraints, but as Gabriele Müller points out, there is now an increasing number of films [and novels] dealing with post-retirement masculinity[2] (and, I should add, also post-retirement femininity) that use traveling as a motif (153) and challenge the master narrative of the young, white male going west. In this context, Janis P. Stout contends that "spatial movement has been the characteristic expression of our sense of life" (4) and argues that the journey narrative is characteristic of American literature: "American history begins with exploration, escape, and home founding. These three are the primary—in the sense of being the earliest and the most basic—patterns of journey narratives in American literature" (30). These patterns have been developed in countless road movies, as David Laderman notes, which deploy the journey as cultural critique (16). In care-home escape stories, the home serves as a starting point to illustrate and reinforce this cultural critique mostly aimed on an abstract level at the ageist cultural narrative of decline, and on a concrete level at the way old people are treated in long-term care facilities.

Oscar Casares' *Amigoland* uses the journey as a motif and employs narrative elements and genre conventions of the road narrative. As will be shown in the following, however, these conventions are turned upside down in nursing home escape stories. This observation leads to the assumption that the reasons for such changes lie in the protagonist's age, which makes it particularly interesting to analyze road narratives especially with regard to this aspect.[3] Why

---

2 | In her essay, Gabriele Müller refers to Paul Mazursky's *Harry and Tonto* (1974), the story of a retired schoolteacher who travels with his cat across the USA, and contrasts it with more recent American movies, *About Schmidt* by Alexander Payne (2002), and David Lynch's *Straight Story* (1999), as well as European interpretations of the road movie, the German film *Schultze Gets the Blues* (2003) by Michael Schorr and the Icelandic film *Children of Nature* by Fridrik Fridriksson (1992) (Müller 150).

3 | In my larger research project "Putting Age into Place" I include other aspects of intersectionality as well to show that especially the intersection of gender and age is relevant for the development of the plot in road novels and movies. For the gendered space of the road, see Alexandra Ganser's

does age matter? What role does age play for the generic conventions of the road narrative? With *Driving Visions* (2002), David Laderman has written an excellent book about the genre, but I disagree with his observation regarding old protagonists in road narratives. Laderman argues,

As we have seen throughout, the genre is born in and through the counterculture, and is driven essentially by *youthful* rebellion against stability, conformity, and tradition. More typically in the road movie, senior citizens signify such stability and tradition, epitomizing the law and home, both in terms of character (harking back to the "old days") and their physical limitations. Driving the genre with an elder senior, therefore, automatically inclines toward sanitizing its culturally critical core. As with road movies featuring children, such a perspective renders the genre more palatable, more family-oriented, more conventional—and less culturally critical. (184)

Although Laderman is right that traditionally the road narrative (he refers exclusively to movies) is a genre associated with young and usually male self-discovery and liberation from the constraints of social expectations, a genre in which characters step outside the social and symbolic order to defamiliarize themselves from convention and conformity (Müller 153), his assumption that the perspective of elders "sanitizes its culturally critical core" means buying into the binary logic of young and old and perpetuates the ageist stereotype of the boring, conventional, homogeneous mass of old people, thereby also marginalizing them and denying their participation not only in social and cultural life, but also in the criticism thereof. Also, it means underestimating the socially critical potential of road narratives that feature old protagonists. In recent years, old men and women have inscribed themselves into the genre without, however, rendering the genre more "palatable" or 'conventional," as Lader-

---

insightful study *Roads of Her Own* as well as Heidi Slettedahl Macpherson's book *Women's Movement: Escape as Transgression in North American Feminist Fiction.*

man puts it. On the contrary, they point to crucial issues regarding self-determination and agency, including the hotly debated issue of long-term care and society's tabooing of death—topics that prevail in recent films and novels.[4] "Driving the road movie with a senior can become a challenge to the genre itself," even if it can entail refreshing perspectives, Laderman argues (184):

"Like that of women, gays, and people of color, this elder perspective becomes an outsider perspective within an outsider genre, a fresh revitalization of the typical young white male point of view of most classic road movies. [...] the genre gets fresh fuel from the new/'old' perspective behind the wheel." (184)

When elderly characters running away from the confinement of institutional care hit the road, the genre's traditions are in fact challenged. Whereas young protagonists flee from conventions and break out of the familiar, old protagonists attempt to reclaim the familiar, their place in society, and fight against the marginalized social role assigned to them (Hartung and Maierhofer 15). This, however, does not make the genre more palatable and conventional—on the contrary. Don Fidencio in *Amigoland* wishes for the "placidity of the home" that, as Bauman notes, "sends the tourist to seek new ad-

---

4 | In the last decade, several nursing home escape novels have been published, among them *The 100-Year-Old Man Who Climbed Out the Window and Disappeared* (Jonasson). The 2009 Swedish novel has been translated into 36 languages and is advertised as "international publishing sensation-over six million copies sold worldwide!" on amazon.com. The 2013 film by Felix Herngren has been shown in over 40 countries. With its more than $ 50 million in revenue, it is said to be the most successful Swedish movie ever (Gustavsson, my translation). North American care home escape novels and films include Janet Hepburn's *Flee, Fly, Flown* (2013), Thom Fitzgerald's movie *Cloudburst* (2011), Sara Gruen's *Water for Elephants* (2006), Todd Johnson's *The Sweet By and By* (2009), Gail Radley's *The Golden Days* (1992), or Andrea Barrett's *The Forms of Water* (1993).

ventures" (30). "The home," Bauman argues in his post-modernist interpretation of the metaphorical pilgrim's journey, "is the place to take off the armour and to unpack—the place where nothing needs to be proved and defended as everything is just there, obvious and familiar" (30). Don Fidencio craves this familiarity, this placidity which he connects with his wish to be "at home" somewhere, anywhere and is "homesick" in the care home: "Homesickness means a dream of *belonging*; to be, for once, *of* the place, not merely *in*" (Bauman 30). In *Amigoland,* the protagonist's "dream of belonging" at the end of his life is finally realized by Don Fidencio after he escapes from the cold and sterile care home and travels from Texas to Mexico.

Oscar Casares' novel starts with Don Fidencio once again plotting escape from *Amigoland,* the eponymous nursing home where he was forced to move by his daughter and son in law after a fall in the yard and an increasing prostate problem, the cause of his occasional incontinence, which worries him immensely. He feels alienated and lonely in Amigoland; obviously, the care home's name bears a certain irony as Don Fidencio does not have a single friend there: "Strangers, all strangers, they had taken everyone he knew and replaced them with strangers. This is where they had sent him to die, with strangers" (Casares 16), he describes his experience. His greatest fear is not the fear of death, but the fear to die among those strangers in a place he has absolutely no connection to. Amigoland is an unfamiliar space for Don Fidencio who complains also about the poor quality of care in the emotionless, impersonal institution. He wishes to spend the last years of his life without professional staff and medication that only keeps him alive, he argues, but not living: "Tell me, why it is that nobody wants me, but nobody wants me to die either," he asks his brother (126). He wishes for a more dignified way of living—and dying—and prays for it day by day: "It was just one more humble request added to the short but growing list of things he prayed for every night: [...] for him to find some way to escape from this prison where they kept him against his will; and for his freedom to come soon, even if it should cost him his life, so long as he didn't die here in this bed, surrounded by so many strange and unfamiliar faces" (10). He does not feel at home in Amigoland, which he repeatedly calls "the prison," and therefore refuses to learn the names of other people, nurses and residents, in the facility. He gives them nicknames based on their characteristics, such as "The One With The Flat Face," (26) "The One Who Always Looks Constipated" (10) "The One Who Cries Like a Dying Calf" (243) to refer to staff and fellow residents. On the one hand, these names reveal his lack of attachment and emphasize the anonymous atmosphere. On the other hand, they help Don Fidencio conceal the fact that he cannot always remember people's names anymore. He is aware of his memory slips (the narration indicates his confusion when sudden flashbacks to an indefinite point in time or dream sequences are interspersed in his narration), a circumstance that reinforces his cynicism and bitterness that stem from his fear of completely losing his independence in the home, ending up as "The Useless One," as he refers to himself (34). His fear of decline is expressed also on the level of space:

Alongside the window that looked onto the patio, one of the aides stood in the center of a U-shaped table and uncovered trays for the residents, all of them twitching in their reclining wheelchairs that were more like upright gurneys. She took a spoonful from the first tray [...] and then a second later the aide had to recover the yellowish dollop that had seeped onto the woman' chin. [...] How long could it be before they moved him over to the U-shaped table where the aides would be feeding him? (15-16).

As in many nursing home narratives, there are spaces that denote a closer proximity to dependency and ultimately death than others. The U-shaped table where people have to be fed is one of them, and the part of the building where "The Ones Who Like To Wander Off" (42) are locked up is another. The nursing home reminds Don Fidencio of his own finitude, and although, or because, he keeps telling himself that he does not feel like being reminded of anything regarding his life, he begins thinking about it: "The other reason he preferred to not look around was that he didn't like thinking about his life, how it used to be, how it was now, and what it would likely become, if God didn't do him the good favor of taking him soon. No matter how much he had lost, or they thought he had lost, he was still alert and understood what was happening to him" (16). That escape is the only solution to Don Fidencio's frustration is foreshadowed by his increasing resistance against the infantilizing treatment in the home. He vehemently struggles against the bib he is forced to wear during meals (13-21), feels deprived of his privacy as there are no locks on bathroom doors (31), fears that he will have to keep the uncomfortable plastic lining on his mattress (17) and that he would soon be put in diapers (339). The care giving procedures that may seem necessary for a large institution's efficiency are understood by Don Fidencio as humiliating and degrading. Such procedures, as Julia Twigg points out, are often found embarrassing as they emphasize the lack of control of one's bodily function and are only directed at the body, not at the person. Such failures "return the person to babyhood and underpin the wider infantilization of clients in the care system," Twigg notes (66). Don Fidencio cannot stand this treatment any longer. Realizing that his struggle from within is futile, he feels that the time has come to take action. As a first step, he begins inspecting his walking frame:

"All four tires, front and back, were made of plastic, but he pressed his thumb into them anyway, same as the men used to do when he drove up to a service station. [...] Then he fiddled with the extensions on the handgrips, first making them longer, then shorter, and finally moving them back to their original position, where they should have stayed all along." (7)

His limited scope of action increasingly frustrates Don Fidencio whose walking frame, no matter how much he fiddles with it, is unsuited as a getaway vehicle.

Ever since being put in the nursing home, dreams about his life, his childhood, and especially his grandfather have begun to haunt Don Fidencio. The home functions as a "memento mori"—reminding him every day that he has only very little time left to clarify the family myth regarding his grandfather's kidnapping by Indians who allegedly brought him from Mexico to the United States as a little boy, where he later founded his family. To do so, however, he would have to return to the place of his grandfather's childhood and go back to his ancestor's roots. This idea is particularly important to Don Fidencio as it would eventually also enable him to make peace with the youngest of his eleven brothers, Don Celestino. Due to the decades-old argument over the true cause of their grandfather's disappearance as well as because of a disagreement in Don Celestino's barbershop years earlier, the brothers have lost sight of each other. Don Fidencio's reminiscing not only increases his wish to reconnect with his younger sibling but also sets a process in motion that Robert N. Butler calls "life review"[5], a process that contains the possibility of coming to terms with past conflicts, of reevaluating and re-narrating them in order to integrate them into a positive life course narrative. This process creates a sudden urge in Don Fidencio to contact Don Celestino, but as he calls him in the middle of the night (his sense of time keeps leaving him), Don Celestino is too slow to get up and pick up the phone. One day, however, Socorro convinces Don Celestino, whom the old dispute also begins to bother, to go and visit Don Fidencio in Amigoland. Don Celestino braces himself up to do go and see his brother in the nursing home. After a short moment Don Fidencio recognizes "The One With The White Hair" as his own brother Celestino and immediately begs him to take him

---

5 | In "The Life Review: An Interpretation of Reminiscence in the Aged," a study published in 1963, Robert N. Butler argues that contrary to prevailing assumptions, reminiscence is not an uncontrolled and "aimless wandering of the mind" (266), but an "intentional effort to recall one's personal life story—the full story or at least large portions—with a goal of bringing new understanding and perspective to the present. Butler's 2010 own review of his article in which he underlines its importance even 50 years later has been published as an appendix to Andrew Achenbaum's biography of Robert N. Butler.

home: "You should take me to live with you. Take your brother from this prison" (125). Don Fidencio feels "stuck" in the nursing home whereas his brother is a "free man."

As he realizes that Don Celestino will not let him live in his house, he begins to plead with him to take him on a road trip to the little Mexican village from where their grandfather had allegedly been kidnapped. For Don Celestino, the kidnapping sounds like a popular folkloristic myth, but Don Fidencio seeks in the story a key to understanding his own existence (Sandick n.p.). Don Celestino's visits give Don Fidencio hope and transform him from a defeatist, cynical old man to an invigorated person with a strong sense of purpose: not only does he increasingly start (day)dreaming of his childhood, but he seems rejuvenated, stops using his walker, fights to get his cane back and secretly practices walking without help—very much to the dismay of the nurses who "had already taken away his three canes" (35) to replace them with a walking frame to prevent him from falling. Don Fidencio, however, interprets their safety measures differently, creating a progress narrative: "They'd seen how much improvement he had made with his therapy and now they were scared that one of these days he would slip out and this time they wouldn't be able to catch up to him. [...] They probably thought he would never get anywhere without the walker. But that showed how much they knew Fidencio Rosales" (173). Unnoticed by the nurses, Don Fidencio gathers strength and vigor and decides that he will not be defeated. The risk Don Fidencio will be taking, that of a road trip to Mexico, is his life-altering counter-narrative to the limitations he experiences in the home.

Fidencio on his part also triggers a new interest in the past in his brother Don Celestino who, since his wife had died half a year earlier, also comes to realize the finiteness of his own very existence. The estranged brothers are reconciled when Celestino undusts his old barbershop equipment and brings it to the nursing home, suggesting to cut Fidencio's hair and thus taking both of them back in time to the day of their childish fight in Celestino's former shop that had separated them ten years earlier. At first, Don Fidencio does not want to hear of having his hair cut, but he finally agrees under the condition that he does not have to sit in a wheelchair during the procedure. Don Celestino fetches a regular chair, realizing that this small but important favor opens up the opportunity for reconciliation with his brother. The barber's mirror here functions as a symbol of looking back into the past: "Don Fidencio stayed quiet for some time, looking into the mirror and watching his brother work, though later he seemed to be gazing at something more distant. [...] 'I can remember some of it.' 'Some of what?' Don Celestino asked, brushing the hair off his brother's shoulder" (135). While Celestino is dedicatedly working on his brother's hair (the procedure is narrated in great detail over five whole pages) they begin to indulge in reminiscences of their childhood in the Rio Grande valley. Their physical proximity reunites the brothers and eliminates any distance. When Don Celestino is finished with his work, Don Fidencio is almost rejuvenated: "He turned toward the larger mirror again and kept gazing into it until he could see the faint traces of a face he had almost forgotten" (138). He reconnects with his own self and sees himself as young and old at the same time. As in many literary texts that deal with old age, the image of the mirror also occurs in *Amigoland*. Whereas looking at one's mirror image is often related to the subject's experience of alienation and disintegration ("the mirror stage of old age," Woodward 60), Don Fidencio is not alienated or repelled by what he sees; on the contrary, he recognizes himself as a young man and is ready to begin the journey of his life.

The rejuvenating effect of the haircut is also felt by Don Celestino who, although he had never even dreamed of cutting hair after selling his business, "was surprised how nimble his fingers were" (133). The brothers' reinvigoration prepares the ground for the quest that is set in motion a few days later when Don Fidencio's dreams intensify and revolve around only two topics: escape from the home (101-03), and the promise he had made to his grandfather to return one day to the *ranchito* in Linares: "Then he said to me, 'Tocayo,' because we were both Fidencio, but he hardly ever called me by my name. 'Tocayo, someday when you are older you should go back and see how things are now, what there is of my ranchito. Tell them I always wanted to go back'" (148). In this scene he identifies with his grandfather, the other "Fidencio," again connecting old and young (both of them have the same name), and returning to his younger self by sticking to the promise of returning to the place of his grandfather's childhood.

While Don Celestino is still skeptical whether Don Fidencio's version of the kidnapping story is accurate, Socorro eventually becomes the catalyst for the final decision to undertake the journey. She also begins to take interest in the trip, not least because she wants to be closer to Don Celestino and, as she argues, his family of which Don Fidencio is the only remaining member. Having left her abusive Mexican husband a while earlier, a liberating move challenging traditional gender roles which her mother and aunt still have not forgiven her, Socorro is proud to be self-sustaining by working in the US. She now dreams of Don Celestino asking her to get married and hopes that the journey will eventually facilitate this decision. When the old story about the grandfather's kidnapping comes up again in the two brothers' conversation, Socorro intervenes and pushes them to finally take a trip to the old *ranchito* in a village near Linares in order to find out whose version of history is to be believed and to finally bury the hatch before it is too late. The wish to go back to his roots suddenly materializes when Don Celestino wakes his brother up from his daydream: "'Andale, Fidencio,' 'Andale to where?' [...] 'I came to take you with me.' 'Remember I called you last night?' he said. 'I told you we were taking the trip to the other side, to Linares. The way Papá Grande wanted you to, remember?'" (201). Still drowsy from his dream, Fidencio complies, grabs his things and escapes with his brother, refusing, however, to take his walker with him.

The two brothers leave the home in a taxi and head to Mexico after picking up Socorro. It is remarkable at this point that in contrast to traditional road narratives, the escape car is not a classical American automobile such as a Buick, a Corvette, or a Thunderbird (Soyka 29), but a taxi, which although it does not seem to limit the characters' individual freedom and self-realization presents a slight adaptation of the myths of liberty and autonomy attached to the car in traditional road narratives. The taxi represents a mediated surrogate form of freedom and individualism. If the car is traditionally read as a status symbol and sign of masculinity and male mobility[6], the taxi—still a car, but driven with the help of others—can be interpreted as symbolic of a loss of control and male power which is corroborated by Don Celestino's "little blue pills [...] vitamins, if she had to know" (97) that he hides wedged behind a hot water bottle in the medicine chest, and by Don Fidencio's difficulty to remember who and when he had last had sex with "before women started treating him as if he were a harmless old creature and what he had once carried between his legs had now shriveled up and fallen off" (116).

Don Fidencio's move towards autonomy is not a fast one but literally a step-by-step process: The walker he left in the home is replaced by a foldable walking stick that Socorro gets for Fidencio. Although there clearly is a progress narrative (from wheelchair to walker to cane to foldable walking stick) and Fidencio remobilizes himself, an embarrassing "accident" during the night causes a delay in their journey. Socorro has to help Fidencio clean up the hotel bed and gets fresh clothes for him. After a two-day adventurous road trip in their taxi across the US-Mexican border to Matamoros they finally arrive at their destination, Linares. At first it seems as if they were unable to locate their grandfather's "Rancho Capote," but when they learn that the house had been renamed decades earlier and is now known as "El Rancho De La Paz" (308), they manage to find their way to the little farm. Place names are significant in the novel: Just like "Amigoland," "El Rancho De La Paz," ("The Ranch of Peace") is telling and foreshadows the novel's ending. Whereas "Amigoland" is a hybrid word, mixing English and Spanish—a language combination Don Fidencio had hated in the nursing home, "El Rancho De La Paz" is only Spanish, Don Fidencio's preferred language, the language in which

---

6 | "For nearly a century [...] the auto has been identified with masculinity and male mobility" (Scharff 166, also quoted in Ganser 17).

he feels at home, a language in which he does not have to "think of the right words before he could open his mouth" (18).

Upon arrival at the *ranchito*, the three travelers are met by Carmen Rosales and her old and confused mother, Mamá Nene, who immediately recognizes the Rosales brothers as family members and is very pleased about their visit. "'We knew that with time you would find your way back [...]. We never stopped from hoping, always waiting for this day,' the old woman said, her voice quivering, [...] 'My father, he always told us that the boy would come back'" (317). Mamá Nene welcomes Don Fidencio like a prodigal son. Although she confuses Don Fidencio with her old uncle, Don Fidencio's grandfather who, she recounts, was kidnapped by Indians as a little boy, Don Fidencio's story about the kidnapping is confirmed; as it turns out, she is his and Don Celestino's second cousin but keeps imagining that her uncle Fidencio—who, as mentioned before, had had the same name—has finally returned from his adventure. She begs him to tell her in great detail what had happened since then. Don Fidencio, realizing that any attempts at clarifying her error would be futile, plays along, eventually telling her that nothing could ever have kept him from returning—which is true for himself as well, so he does not lie when he says, "[a]nd this I told them from the beginning, that we needed to go, no matter what, that it was important, that I had made a promise to come back. If they'd let me, I would have walked all the way here" (314). He complies with her wish and begins to tell the whole story, once more identifying with his grandfather. Closing his eyes, he claims that more and more details would be coming back to him, and it is not quite clear at this point what he actually remembers from his grandfather's narration and what he is making up as he goes along. However, when he recounts that the Indians only let him—the little boy—free because he had wet his pants and smelled really bad (329), readers are led to doubt the accuracy of the narration. At this point of the story, the differentiation between factual accuracy and "truth" is irrelevant for both Mamá Nene and Don Fidencio; memories, wishes, dreams, and life review merge: "He had made up so many things he couldn't say where the truth ended and the less-truthful parts began, so that with time it all became the same to him" (340). The story creates a strong bond of familiarity between Mamá Nene and Don Fidencio. When it is time to return to the city, Mamá Nene encourages the travelers to stay overnight. While Don Celestino and Socorro prefer to go back to their hotel, Don Fidencio for whom the return trip feels too exhausting happily accepts the offer to spend the night at El Rancho De La Paz.

Awakening the next morning, Don Fidencio realizes that he feels happy: first of all, he has not wet the bed, and secondly, he is—other than in the nursing home—allowed to smoke a morning cigarette in the bathroom. Most importantly, however, he feels at home. Carmen brings him a cup of coffee out into the garden, and he decides that El Rancho De La Paz is where he belongs:

Earlier the granddaughter had made him some huevos a la mexicana with just enough chiles and spices that he realized he had forgotten what a real breakfast was supposed to taste like. She wasn't his granddaughter, he realized, but her name had gotten away from him again, and in any case, she treated him like he imagined a granddaughter might treat a grandfather. Just yesterday evening when they had already left the store, it had occurred to her to turn the truck around and go back so she could buy him a pack of cigarettes, just in case he ran out in the middle of the night. And this morning after his breakfast, she had brought the coffee to where he was sitting outside, smoking. (350–51)

As opposed to the nursing home where he had to wait until someone unlocked the patio so he could have a smoke after which he had to wait an hour to be let into the mess hall where the same breakfast was served every day ("Monday, oatmeal and raisins. Tuesday, oatmeal and raisins. Wednesday, oatmeal and raisins. On and on that way" 25) and where he constantly looked at "pastel paintings on a pastel wall" (33), where he was forced to wear diapers at night and a bib during meals, he now enjoys his freedom. He is free to walk wherever and whenever he wants to, to smoke on the toilet, and to sit outside in the shade where he enjoys his cup of morning coffee.

From his chair in the garden he looks up "past the first forty feet of the trunk, as the branches became more dense and entangled, eventually blocking out most of the rising sun and leaving only a narrow passageway to see where the sky opened up" (351), which may be read as a metaphorical pathway mapping out his next journey.

The next day, Don Celestino comes back to pick his brother up for their return trip, but Don Fidencio refuses to go: "He realized that it was only by a miracle of God that he was so far away from that place and all those strangers. And really, how many miracles could one old man expect to have?" (341).

Don Fidencio's quest is successful regarding three aspects: he has fulfilled the promise he had made to his grandfather to go back to Mexico, he has escaped institutional confinement, and he has found himself a new home where he can die in dignity and peace. This motivation of "the home-founding journey," a common pattern in American quest narratives, as Janice P. Stout argues in *The Journey Narrative in American Literature,* joins the "exploration and escape" pattern as well as the "journey home" motif that she also determines. After his escape, Don Fidencio has literally arrived "at home." Carmen and Mamá Nene invite Don Fidencio to stay with them for good, and he happily accepts their offer. Don Fidencio informs his daughter Amalia about his decision to stay in Mexico. As expected, she argues with him, promising him that he could stay with her and her husband, but he knows that his daughter's promise would not last very long. "Suddenly I have so many places to live—everybody wants me for themselves," Don Fidencio states not without a hint of bitterness (354). Don Celestino, asking his brother about the reason for his decision, receives a very simple answer: "Just to live in peace" (254). He realizes that he cannot possibly convince Don Fidencio to change his mind and says good-bye. Leaving the ranch in his taxi, Don Celestino discovers the plastic bag with Don Fidencio's medication: "But when Don Celestino looked inside the bag, the pill dispenser was still packed and the extra vials hadn't been opened. Everything was the same as it was when they left the pharmacy five days earlier" (357). Don Fidencio not only leaves his walker but also his entire medication behind in the car. The book ends without absolute closure but suggests that the circle of Don Fidencio's life is coming to a close. Narrating his story, he has finished his "life review."

Why Carmen agrees to take care of a person she barely knows remains open; there is neither a hint of her altruism in the story nor of money being offered that leads to this agreement. Her openness is explained merely on the basis of cultural difference and in opposition to the capitalist US system. Even if Carmen accepts Don Fidencio's understandable wish to die in peace not among strangers but with his family, this wish is sentimentalized and transferred to an almost mythical level as he actually does not know the Rosales family he is staying with at all. The ranch, an idyllic place where past and present converge, can be interpreted as what Mikhail Bakhtin theorizes as "the idyllic chronotope in the novel." Bakhtin's idyllic chronotope offers an explanation for the conclusion otherwise difficult to understand, given Don Fidencio's old age and need for care: "Strictly speaking, the idyll does not know the trivial details of everyday life" (Bakhtin 226). Bakhtin, in introducing the term "chronotope," refers to a converging of time and space, or, as Heike Hartung puts it, "translates spatial simultaneity into temporal sequence, thus localising time in concrete space" (8). Bakhtin explains that it is the idyll itself (in the case of *Amigoland*, "El Rancho De La Paz") that constitutes the chronotope:

The unity of the life of generations (in general, the life of men) in an idyll is in most instances primarily defined by the *unity of place*, by the age-old rooting of the life of generations to a single place, from which this life, in all its events, is inseparable. This unity of place in the life of generations weakens and renders less distinct all the temporal boundaries between individual lives and between various phases of one and the same life. The unity of place brings together and even fuses the cradle and the grave (the same little corner, the same earth) and brings together as well childhood and old age (the same grove, stream, the same lime trees, the same house), the life of the various generations who had also lived in that same place, under the same conditions, and who had seen the same things. (225)

Looking at El Rancho de La Paz from a Bakhtinian perspective, the novel's ending is plausible and stands in a long tradition of the idyllic family novel.

Amigoland is not only a quest narrative but also a "Vollendungsroman," a novel of completion, of "winding up," as Constance Rooke calls it in her essay "Old Age in Contemporary Fiction. A New Paradigm of Hope" (245), a genre concerned with the last stages of life which entails letting go and finding "some kind of affirmation in the face of loss" (248). Life review is one of the most common themes of the "Vollendungsroman." Don Fidencio undertakes such a life review and undertakes the quest to reclaim his dignity in old age. Andrew Achenbaum, with reference to Robert N. Butler, describes the process as follows:

> Some of the positive results of a life review can be the righting of old wrongs, making up with enemies, coming to accept one's own mortality, gaining a sense of serenity, pride in accomplishment and a feeling of having done one's best. Life review gives people an opportunity to decide what to do with the time left to them and work out emotional and material legacies. People become ready to die. (204)

Don Fidencio's quest is successful in that it fulfills the aspects addressed by Andrew Achenbaum. He reclaims what he considers essential at the end of life and undertakes the road trip to reclaim his dignity. The journey is a journey into his past and his future at the same time, a "blurring of all the temporal boundaries," as Bakhtin puts it (225), a necessary trip to bring his life to an end, albeit in a somewhat folkloristic way, in the home of his ancestors. Heather Gardiner explains the necessity of the journey back as follows:

> Through retrospect, the wheel of life is turned back to youth and childhood and in many instances, but not all, new pathways are opened towards a different kind of homecoming. The old person ends the journey of life where he or she began it, seeing its full span with a perspective which is only possible

when age restricts the physical momentum of life and the journey comes "full circle" in some yet "untrodden" pathways of the mind. (59-60)

Don Fidencio's journey also comes back "full circle" to the place his grandfather—or, in his version of the story which fuses his grandfather's with his own identity—he himself, had left. He establishes a sense of unity by bringing together the events of his life into a whole, creating a sense of completion for himself. He has fulfilled his goals, kept his promise, and found a place where he finds peace—the idyllic "Racho De La Paz"—where he will be taken care of until the very end of his days by people he now considers family. From the nightmarish institution Don Fidencio escapes into a fairy tale-like "and they lived happily ever after" setting.

In some care home novels, protagonists who experience the physical sense of confinement and entrapment in old age react by "initiating an exploration into the distant memories in the attic of the mind," as Gardiner metaphorically puts it (57). Don Fidencio's journeys—the physical journey he undertakes to travel from Texas to Mexico as well as the imaginary journey in his grandfather's name—put Mamá Nene at rest as she, also at the end of her life, can stop waiting for the return of "her uncle." Furthermore, the journeys facilitate Don Fidencio's life review and enable him to re-narrate his life story, to come to terms with his Mexican-American identity and bring the journey of his life to a positive conclusion.

Questions of space and place in the novel, however, also play out on a larger scale. By pitting Mexico against the US and the family against the institution, the idyllic narration here suggests that "blood is thicker than water" and buys into the problematic ideology that ethnicity is based on blood and soil. The narration adopts the common narrative that even modern Mexican culture is a culture where families traditionally take care of their elders until the end of their lives.[7] This binary opposition is represented in the story not

---

7 | Eldercare in Mexico is largely carried out by families, i.e. women caregivers, but due to social and demographic change, care homes will be

only by Carmen Rosales and Mamá Nene but also by Socorro who lives across the border in Matamoros with her mother and aunt, "still cooking and cleaning and shopping and going to the pharmacy for these pills or that salve that her mother might need" (81). Her mother and her old aunt are worried about Socorro eventually getting married to the "old American" which for them would entail losing their own family caregiver. They advise her to look for another house to clean in order to stop seeing him. Socorro's mother and aunt expect Socorro to adhere to normative femininity associated with home, hearth, and family as well as traditional patterns in terms of caregiving, and Socorro, a woman of the borderlands traveling back and forth across the border and feeling at home at both sides, is presented as breaking with traditional gender roles.

The novel with its passionate indictment of the institutionalization of the aged is ambivalent in its juxtaposition of tradition and modernity. While Socorro struggles against her family's expectations to be their care-giver, *Amigoland* makes the deficits of institutional care, respectively the fears and anxieties of its recipients, very explicit. It mirrors the criticism already voiced in famous nursing home ethnographies such as Jaber F. Gubrium's *Living and Dying at Murray Manor* (1975) and *Speaking of Life* (1993), in Timothy Diamond's *Making Gray Gold* (1992), in *The Culture of Long Term Care* (1995) edited by J. Neil Henderson and Maria D. Vesperi, or in *Gray*

---

needed, a challenge which has been recognized by social scientists and policymakers. As Robledo et al. state in their article "The State of Elder Care in Mexico" (2012), "[c]urrently, the majority of the older population lives at home with their spouse or partner, children, grandchildren or other close relatives. Here, most of the long-term care they need is provided to them and within this pool of family members, mostly by women. Nevertheless, reduced fertility rates, constant rural-urban migration within Mexico and international migration, women' s increasing participation in the labor force and activities outside the home, among other factors, have changed family size and composition and pose future challenges to the availability of household care and support" (187).

Areas: Ethnographic Encounters with Nursing Home Culture edited by Philip B. Stafford. As Oscar Casares states in an interview, the story is based on his own personal experience with his ninety year-old father who fell and broke his hip, which led to him spending the last three years of his life in a nursing home, an experience that was "possibly one of the most difficult for [the] family" (Casares 8). Despite its idyllic and at times sentimental overtones, the novel also criticizes institutional problems and illustrates what good end-of-life care means. Told largely from the point of view of Don Fidencio, the novel allows readers to empathize with the protagonist which might eventually contribute to outcomes "of changed attitudes, improved motives, and better care and justice," as Susan Keen writes in "A Theory of Narrative Empathy" (208). Qualities such as privacy, intimacy, friendship, community, and warmth, as Don Fidencio would wish for, are not taken care of in the American institution but in Mexico where a "family member" acts as the main caregiver. Carmen and El Rancho De La Paz epitomize the binary opposite of "Amigoland" which does not focus on relationship-centered care. In this regard, Oscar Casares's novel does not facilitate an imagination of institutional care that could fend off the nursing home specter. The care home is a place to be avoided at all cost—as Don Fidencio states: "It was just one more humble request added to the short but growing list of things he prayed for every night [...], for his freedom to come soon, even if it should cost him his life" (10). While the context of the home suggests isolation, dependency, inability, infantilization, boredom, frailty, and very limited agency in confinement, the concept of "traveling" implies movement, change of location, independence, agency, freedom, and choice. *Amigoland* illustrates Don Fidencio's journey to freedom which grants him dignity at the end of his days. By finding a place where he feels at home and at peace despite his physical ailments, he does not exemplify what is commonly seen as "successful aging," but what Wendy Lustbader terms "successful frailty":

Turning the "nothing" of empty time into the "something" of good days is the alchemy of successful frailty. At first, having too much time on our hands can feel like a daily humiliation in our making so little of it. Waiting for help emphasizes all the dignities and freedoms that have been ripped away from us. Gradually, if we do not become hardened in our disappointment, we can turn the insults of illness into privileges of being. (15)

It is in this sense that Don Fidencio ages successfully; his need for care, his dependence, is redefined as "successful frailty" at El Rancho De La Paz through Mamá Nene and Carmen. Successful frailty, I would argue, is of central importance to the genre of the "Vollendungsroman" and the stage of disengagement, "of leaving the social stage," as Rooke describes it (245). "The task of the Vollendungsroman is to discover for its protagonist and for the reader some kind of affirmation in the face of loss" (248), she argues. This is also true for Don Fidencio as a "senior tourist" facing the end of his life's journey.

Works Cited

Achenbaum, Andrew. *Robert N. Butler, MD: Visionary of Healthy Aging*: Columbia University Press, 2013. Print.

Bakhtin, Mikhail M. "Forms of Time and Chronotope in the Novel. Notes toward a Historical Poetics." *The Dialogic Imagination: Four Essays*. Ed. Michael Holquist. Austin: University of Texas Press, 1981 (1937-38). 84-258. Print.

Barrett, Andrea. *The Forms of Water*. New York: Washington Square Press, 1993. Print.

Bauman, Zygmunt. "From Pilgrim to Tourist: A Short History of Identity." *Questions of Cultural Identity*. Ed. Stuart Hall and Paul Du Gay. London, Thousand Oaks, Calif. Sage, 1996. 18-36. Print.

Butler, Robert N. "The Life Review: An Interpretation of Reminiscence in the Aged." *New Thoughts on Old Age*. Ed. Robert Kastenbaum. Berlin, Heidelberg: Springer, 1964. 265-80. Print.

Casares, Oscar. *Amigoland*. 1st ed. Boston, Mass: Back Bay Books, 2009. Print.

Chivers, Sally. "On the Road Again: Aritha Van Herk's *No Fixed Address* and Suzette Mayr's *The Widows.*" *Adventures of the Spirit: The Older Woman in the Works of Doris Lessing, Margaret Atwood, and Other Contemporary Women Writers.* Ed. Phyllis S. Perrakis. Columbus: Ohio State University Press, 2007. 200-15. Print.

Cole, Thomas R. *The Journey of Life: A Cultural History of Aging in America.* Cambridge: Cambridge University Press, 1992. Print.

Diamond, Timothy. *Making Gray Gold: Narratives of Nursing Home Care.* Chicago: University of Chicago Press, 1992. Print.

Fitzgerald, Thom, dir. *Cloudburst*. Perf. Brenda Fricker and Olympia Dukakis. Thom Fitzgerald, 2011. DVD.

Friðriksson, Friðrik Þór, dir. *Children of Nature.* Perf. Gísli Halldórsson and Sigriður Hagalín. Friðrik Þ. Friðriksson, 1991. DVD.

Ganser, Alexandra. *Roads of Her Own: Gendered Space and Mobility in American Women's Road Narratives, 1970-2000.* Amsterdam, New York, NY: Rodopi, 2009. Print.

Gardiner, Heather. "The Portrayal of Old Age in English-Canadian Fiction." PhD dissertation. *University of Toronto*, 1998. Web. 6 September 2013. <http://www.worldcat.org/oclc/46551235>.

Goffman, Erving. *Asylums: Essays on the Social Situation of Mental Patients and Other Inmates.* 1st ed. Garden City, N.Y. Anchor Books, 1961. Print.

Gruen, Sara. *Water for Elephants: A Novel.* Toronto: Harper Perennial, 2007. Print.

Gubrium, Jaber F. *Speaking of Life: Horizons of Meaning for Nursing Home Residents.* Hawthorne, N.Y: Aldine de Gruyter, 1993. Print.

—. *Living and Dying at Murray Manor.* Expanded pbk. ed. Charlotteville: University Press of Virginia, 1997. Print.

Gustavsson, Matilda. "Nytt rekord för 'Hundraåringen'." *DN.KULTUR* 23 Jul. 2014, Online: n.p. Web. 14 Aug. 2014. <http://www.dn.se/kultur-noje/film-tv/nytt-rekord-for-hundraaringen/>.

Hartung, Heike, and Roberta Maierhofer. "Introduction." *Narratives of Life: Mediating Age*. Ed. Heike Hartung and Roberta Maierhofer. Vienna: Lit, 2009. 5-18. Print.

Hartung, Heike. "Narrating Age." Habilitationsschrift. *Universität Potsdam*, 2013. Print.

Henderson, J. N., and Maria D. Vesperi, eds. *The Culture of Long Term Care: Nursing Home Ethnography*. Westport, Conn. [u.a.]: Bergin & Garvey, 1995. Print.

Hepburn, Janet. *Flee, Fly, Flown*. Toronto: Second Story Press, 2013. Print.

Herngren, Felix, dir. *The Hundred-Year-Old Man Who Climbed Out the Window and Disappeared*. Perf. Robert Gustafsson. Film i Väst, 2013. DVD.

Johnson, Todd. *The Sweet By And By*. New York: HarperCollins, 2009. Print.

Jonasson, Jonas. *The Hundred-Year-Old Man Who Climbed Out Of The Window And Disappeared*. London: Hyperion, 2012. Print.

Keen, Suzanne. "A Theory of Narrative Empathy." Narrative 14.3 (2006): 207-36. Web. <http://content.epnet.com/ContentServer.asp?T=P&P=AN&K=21644604&EbscoContent=dGJyMMTo50SeqLc4v%2BvlOLCmroyep7VSsKe4TLaWxWXS&ContentCustomer=dGJyMPGotoiora9LuePfgeyx%2BEu3q64A&D=aph>.

Laderman, David. *Driving Visions: Exploring the Road Movie*. 1st ed. Austin: University of Texas Press, 2002. Print.

Lynch, David, dir. *The Straight Story*. Perf. Richard Farnsworth, Sissy Spacek, and Harry D. Stanton. Walt Disney Pictures et al., 1999. DVD.

Lustbader, Wendy. *Counting On Kindness: The Dilemmas of Dependency*. New York, Toronto: Simon & Schuster, 1991. Print.

Mazursky, Paul, dir. Harry and Tonto. Perf. Art Carney, Herbert Berghof, and Ellen Burstyn. Paul Mazursky, 1974. DVD.

Macpherson, Heidi S. *Women's Movement: Escape as Transgression in North American Feminist Fiction*. Amsterdam: Rodopi, 2000. Print. Costerus 128.

Müller, Gabriele. "The Aged Traveler: Cinematic Representations of Post-Retirement Masculinity." *Narratives of Life: Mediating Age*. Ed. Heike Hartung and Roberta Maierhofer. Vienna: Lit, 2009. 149-65. Print.

Payne, Alexander, dir. *About Schmidt*. Perf. Jack Nicholson. Michael Besman and Harry Gittes, 2002. DVD.

Radley, Gail. *The Golden Days*. New York: Puffin Books, 1992. Print.

Robledo, Luis Miguel Gutiérrez, Mariana López Ortega, and Victoria Eugenia Arango Lopera. "The State of Elder Care in Mexico." *Current Translational Geriatrics and Experimental Gerontology Reports* 1.4 (2012): 183-89. Print.

Rooke, Constance. "Old Age in Contemporary Fiction. A New Paradigm of Hope." *Handbook of the Humanities and Aging*. Ed. Thomas R. Cole, David van Tassel, and Robert Kastenbaum. 1st ed. New York: Springer Pub., 1992. 241-57. Print.

Sandick, Phil. *Amigoland, by Oscar Casares: Book Review*. Fiction Writers Review, 2010. Web. 24 August 2014. <http://fictionwritersreview.com/review/amigoland-by-oscar-casares/>.

Scharff, Virginia. *Taking the Wheel: Women and the Coming of the Motor Age*. 1st pbk. ed. Albuquerque: University of New Mexico Press, 1992. Print.

Schorr, Michael, dir. *Schultze Gets the Blues*. Perf. Horst Krause, Harald Warmbrunn, and Karl-Fred Müller. Jens Körner, 2003. DVD.

Soyka, Amelie. *Raum und Geschlecht: Frauen im Road Movie der 90er Jahre*. Frankfurt am Main, New York: Peter Lang, 2002. 37. Print.

Stafford, Philip B. *Gray Areas: Ethnographic Encounters With Nursing Home Culture*. 1st ed. Santa Fe, Oxford: School of American Research Press; James Currey, 2003. Print.

Stout, Janis P. *The Journey Narrative in American Literature: Patterns and Departures*. Westport, Conn. Greenwood Press, 1983. Print.

Twigg, Julia. "The Body, Gender, and Age: Feminist Insights in Social Gerontology." *Journal of Aging Studies* 18.1 (2004): 59-73. Print.

Uteng, Tanu P., and Tim Cresswell, eds. *Gendered Mobilities*. Aldershot, England, Burlington, VT: Ashgate, 2008. Print.

Woodward, Kathleen M. "Instant Repulsion: Decrepitude, The Mirror Stage, and The Literary Imagination." *Kenyon Review* 5.4 (1983): 43-66. Web. <http://search.ebscohost.com/login.aspx?direct=true&db=aph&AN=10891837&site=ehost-live>.

"(Un)Comfortably Moving Out of the Comfort Zone: Life as Travel"

Roberta Maierhofer

Representations of travel and mobility are important cultural narratives expressing issues and concerns of postmodern identity. In this paper, narratives of movement and changing of place will be discussed as existential expressions of the experience of time and place. Vilém Flusser's concept of the *expelled* and Zygmunt Bauman's notions of *pilgrim, stroller, vagabond,* and *tourist* position processes of temporary and permanent exclusion (and possible inclusion) that can be defined and re-defined as normative human experience where transcendence and impermanence are recognized as an essential human condition expressed in the need for physical movement. While Flusser discusses this on the level of exile, Bauman sketches changes of perception in the movement "From Pilgrim to Tourist," as stated in the title of his analysis. Relevant for the aspect of travel and tourism is the relationship between the familiar and the strange, between self and other, between movement and identity. Flusser states the importance of constantly seeking the other in order to define the self:

But this is not the decisive part of the discovery that we are not trees—that the uprooted make history. Instead, the decisive part is to discover how tiresome it is not to establish new roots. [...] To continue to experience expulsion, which is to say: to allow oneself to be expelled again and again. (Flusser 4)

Flusser continues to express the importance of a constant changing of positions, both for those that move as well as for those that remain in one place:

> The expelled is the other of others. Which is to say, he is other for the others, and the others are other for him. He himself is nothing more than the others of him. In this manner, he is able to "identify." His advent in exile allows the original natives to uncover that they are unable to "identify" without him. Because of this advent in exile, the "self" is rent asunder, opening it up to others, to a being-with-others. This dialogic atmosphere that characterizes exile is not necessarily part of a mutual recognition, but rather, it is mostly polemical (not to mention murderous). (Flusser 9)

Flusser links aspects of migration and exile to creativity, and the importance of any society for renewal:

> For the expelled threatens the "particular nature" of the original natives; this strangeness calls him into question. But, even such a polemical dialogue is creative; for it leads to the synthesis of new information. Exile, no matter what form it takes, is a breeding ground for creative activity, for the new. Being expelled means being forced to become other, and to be other than the others. Therefore this is not only about a geographic phenomenon: one is somewhere else after the expellation. This is also about a phenomenon of freedom: one is forced to be creative. In this sense the equation expellation=creation may be turned around: Not only is every expelled forced to be creative, but also everyone who is creative sees himself forced to be expelled. (Flusser 9)

Movements through space and time within a life course are expressions of conscious acts of appropriation. American literature provides many examples of narratives of identity where travel and movement only make an expression of time possible. Moving through space—the postmodern "problem of identity," as Bauman has stated, as the avoidance of fixation and keeping options of identity open, only makes an expression of time and experience possible, and is therefore all about age. Thus, through the narrations of these experiences of travel and escape can be enabled—to use Bauman's words—from the limits that each society sets to "life strategies that can be imagined." (Bauman, 36) The narrative reflections of changed spaces and strange contexts allow for an expression of the fluidity of one's identity, and thus open up possibilities of moving beyond defined positions of self. If identity is defined by both continuity and change over a life course, the importance is to narrate one's life in an on-going process of dialogue between the strange and the familiar. (Un)comfortably moving out of the comfort zone—whether as expelled or tourist—is then expressed as an existential experience of life.

Since the 1980s, scholars in the field of cultural gerontology have turned to cultural manifestations to investigate ideas about the meaning of identity within the life course, and discuss models of aging presented in literature, art, and film. Within the interplay between the fields of science and the humanities, textual representations are important sources that contribute towards understanding "identity in movement," the matrix of time and experience within the many contexts in which a person moves over the duration of a life. Examining reactions to personal crises and turning points as expressed in cultural representations provides researchers with unique insights into the way individuals construct their lives. Sociologists have suggested that narratives or stories play a central part in the construction of lives, as what is meaningful about ourselves is expressed through the telling of stories. Whereas on the public level these stories communicate the significance of particular lives and communities for society as a whole, on the individual level the telling of stories is a medium for the integration of lives, for explaining discontinuities as well as continuities. Fluidity of identity opens up possibilities of moving beyond a defined position of self, and makes it not only possible but necessary to view personal and institutional structures as well as relationships in new ways. If identity is defined by both continuity and change over a life course, the importance is not only to narrate one's life, but also to interpret these narrations in an on-going process of dialogue not only between cultural representations and the interpretations of these, but also between generations to establish an intergenerational discourse as well as between the various disciplines to charter an interdisciplinary approach to time and experience. Narrating physical movement as a traveler and tourist at all stages of one's life as an expression of the movement of time and the experience of both the familiar and the strange, the self and the other offers a platform for such communication.

American literature with its emphasis on the individual—early on identified by Alexis de Tocqueville as America's specific ideology—includes many texts which show the difficulties of becoming oneself, the difficulties resulting from the social pressure to conform. Nina Baym speaks of James Fenimore Cooper's frontiersman Natty Bumppo as the archetypal representation of an American identity and the prototypical American hero. (Baym, Making, 220) In American Studies the cultural narrative of the quest of the individual for a self-determined life in opposition to the norms of society is linked to travel, journey, and the presence of landscape and nature—all aspects that play an important role in tourism. Mark Twain's *The Adventures of Huckleberry Finn* (1885) or James Fenimore Cooper's *Leather-Stocking Tales* can be read as expressions of regional identities situated in a certain time and space within a very specific geography, but for the many readers over the centuries it has also offered the possibility of envisioning not only a looking back in time, but an experience of space. On the level of such literary texts defining a cultural and national identity, Huck Finn and Natty Bumppo—heroes despite themselves—embody the issue of democracy, an understanding that the rights of the individual have to be protected and encouraged in order to guarantee self-expression as part of the very specific American identity. Road trips both in novels and films express this notion that travel and mobility are expressions of individualism and freedom—cultural narratives so embedded in US American imagination and fueled by constant re-imagination, construction, deconstruction and reconstruction. Not surprisingly, when feminist literary scholarship in the late 1970s turned to an analysis of female experience and perspectives, Nina Baym's scorching criticism of the bias of American literary criticism for all things male, juxtaposed a ship (even if this was not a cruise liner but Herman Melville's whaling ship in *Moby Dick*) as a metaphor with sewing circles—very much home-based and in place. (Baym, *Women's Fiction*) The American cultural narrative of personal identity has been formative of the study of American literature. Since the mid-1970s, the prototypical American male protagonist with his quest for self as a rebel against societal pressure has been supplemented by the female hero. Feminist literary criticism reclaimed the female hero of traditional literature and reinterpreted her in the light of feminist analysis, and the female protagonist sets off on her own journey of adventure and self-discovery. Since the mid-1980s, it is the aging female protagonist who—no longer the mocked figure of conventionality and comic relief—is seen as now claiming space as the female counter-part to the male hero, a tourist in her own right. By moving out of their comfort zones in terms of spatial movement, these aging female protagonists now position themselves in the center, become more self-confident and self-decisive in their encounters with the outer world, and feel themselves in a position to make decisions that are usually not approved of by family and friends. It is a step from silence to narration, from negating to accepting one's own feelings and needs. Through physical travel, mental movement becomes possible. By turning towards the self, the protagonists find the strength, to express the self for the outer world. These women are forced to look back on their previous lives and define their own points of view. An integral part of this revision is a confrontation with their own passivity, their own failures. These women often can be faulted for not having taken action, for having repressed their own wishes and needs in favor of others. By coping with their past, these protagonists define their present and open up for possibilities in the future. The starting point of this revision is often a feeling of helplessness in view of the momentary situation, the inability to imagine a solution to their problems. This state of mind is presented as static, depressing and without perspectives for the future. Movement of the body, however, makes movement of the mind possible.

In Grace Paley's short story "The Long-Distance Runner," the ambiguities and ambivalences of the self are expressed in the ironic distancing of the narrator from her own life, which one critic referred to as her "Pollyannaism." (Mandel, 94) The protagonist Faith—stout and forty-two—jogs out to explore the urban streets beyond her Greenwich Village neighborhood and ventures into a world no longer familiar to her. At the beginning of the short story her decision to become a long-distance runner is linked to changes both within herself—her own aging—and changes of her environment—urban renewal. She becomes a tourist within her own context, and thus recognizes the familiar as strange, and the strange as familiar:

One day, before or after forty-two, I became a long-distance runner. Though I was stout and in many ways inadequate to this desire, I wanted to go far and fast, not as fast as bicycles and trains, not as far as Taipei, Hingwen, places like that, islands of the slant-eyed cunt, as sailors in bus stations say when speaking of travel, but round and round the country from the sea side to the bridges, along the old neighborhood streets a couple of times, before old age and urban renewal ended them and me. (Paley, 179)

No longer passive, the narrator has to keep moving:

I wanted to stop and admire the long beach. I wanted to stop in order to think admiringly about New York. There aren't many rotting cities so tan and sandy and speckled with citizens at their salty edges. But I had already spent a lot of life lying down or standing and staring, I had decided to run. (Paley, 181)

Faith sprints through the city streets to her former neighborhood in Coney Island, once Jewish, now black, and ends up in the tenement building in which she was raised. Returning home after having lived for three weeks with a black family that now inhabits the apartment she grew up in, she is faced with her family's inability to comprehend the changes she has induced. She herself, however, is satisfied with the simplicity of her motivation:

> Because it isn't usually so simple. Have you known it to happen much nowadays? A woman inside the steamy energy of middle age runs and runs. She finds the houses and streets where her childhood happened. She lives in them. She learns as though she was still a child what in the world is coming next. (Paley, 198)

Whereas her childhood "happened"—aging is linked to movement and passion: "A woman inside the steamy energy of middle age runs and runs." The ironic almost absurd narrative has been linked by critics to the tradition of remembering, of telling stories, a purposeful, somewhat defiant act. (Aarons, 30) Jacqueline Taylor compares the narrative structure of Paley's short stories to the structure of women's personal narratives, which recount women's experiences in a non-linear, open-ended story. Paley interviewed at the age of fifty-eight, almost ten years after the short story was published, when asked about her "images of older, freer women" equates aging with empowerment:

> I think that in almost any culture the older women really begin to have a certain power. So, I'm getting older, so I really feel freer than I ever felt. I probably will feel even more so. I think some of it comes from being part of a movement but some of it comes really from just getting older and also making my own living. (Todd, 38)

As the well-used metaphor of journey for the life-course indicates, physical movement is as such an act of liberation from confining social boundaries. Grace Paley's short story can be read as a conscious act of acceptance of her own aging. The concept of the search for identity as a heroic quest, it is through the aspect of female gender that we as readers—both female and male—can envision a world where this dichotomy is overcome. Analyzing the aspect of the female heroic journey, Pearson and Pope come to the following conclusion:

> Indeed, the female hero learns a series of paradoxical truths. Self and other, mind and body, spirit and flesh, male and female, are not necessarily in opposition to one another. The hero's reward for violating the sex-role taboos of her society is the miracle of combining inner wholeness with outward community. Such a shift of consciousness cannot be taught; it can only be achieved. The hero learns about paradox by journeying through duality. (Pearson, Pope, 15)

In the novel *Praisesong for the Widow* by Paule Marshall, this "journeying through duality" is experienced by Avey Avatara Johnson, a 64-year-old middle-class widow cruising the Caribbean with two friends, when she suddenly decides to disembark on the Caribbean island Grenada in order to fly back to New York City. The decision to return home is motivated by torturing nightmares, in which her great aunt Cuney appears and summons her with ever increasing urgency to Tatem, the island where she used to spend the summer as a child. When she misses her flight back to New York, she spends the night in a hotel, where she experiences hallucinations aroused by conflicting dreams, memories and visions, and where she confronts her rage and grief at having wasted a life in pursuit of material wealth, and she is finally able to mourn her husband, whom she lost long before his actual death, when he decided to assimilate and dedicate his life to success and upward mobility. The next day she meets an old man, Lebert Joseph, who tells her about the "Carriacou Excursion," an annual island festival honoring the long-time ancestors and he convinces her to accompany him on the trip. This meeting of the out-island people with family roots on the island represents in its rituals and myths a connection to the past and the original African tradition. The ceremony of the great drums, for example, stands for a revival of the spiritual powers of the African past. Through the journey to Carriacou and the intensive experience of the dance ritual and the music Avey Johnson discovers her own identity as an

American of African descent. After this experience, she decides to return home with a mission to teach the next generation the importance of the past as a basis for a definition of one's identity in the present, to rediscover the spiritual home of her ancestors in Tatem, South Carolina, and thus take on the role of her great aunt Cuney for the next generation. Avey Johnson's spiritual orientation and the rediscovered power to become socially active is won in almost ritual steps. (Reyes, 186-7) While at the beginning of her marriage, Avey cultivates the simple rituals of her cultural heritage, such as Afro-American music and poetry, dancing and their visits to Tatem, and recognizes and savors these aspects of her life as sustaining and valuable for her existence, the knowledge of the importance of these rituals is lost when she and her husband determine their lives according to the American dream of material success and social upward mobility. Angelita Reyes speaks in this context of the loss of cultural orientation and the spiritual death of both Avey and her husband ("they had died on the killing ground of materialism and false cultural values") (Reyes, 189) Reyes convincing interpretation that Avey achieves through the ritual act of cleansing and rebirth self-confidence concerning her cultural identity, should, however, be supplemented by the importance of the physical aspect.

It is the aspect of physical movement that initiates recognition of her own physicality. Avey's definition of self takes place in the conscious acceptance of her aging, which occurs in a new awareness of her own body, and this process can only be initiated through her travel. Both Reynes and Linda Pannill emphasize the detailed narration of physical aspects in the novel as pivotal, such as the vomiting and defecating of the sea-sick Avey during the journey to Carriacou Island, where she recalls her girlhood journeys to Tatem and her neighborhood's annual outing on the Hudson to Bear Island. At that stage in her life, she had felt invisible threads as strong as the lifelines at Coney Island, connecting the hearts and navels of everyone boarding. The rough journey by water also brings to mind the Middle Passage and the watery rocking of the womb. Avey remembers from her childhood a sermon one Easter Sunday when the church seemed to rock in the hands of God until she was sick to her stomach. As a grown woman she becomes sick on the small boat, but this sickness is purgative. An oppressive heaviness long vaguely felt is relieved. Similar to Avey's physical reaction to the dreams of her great aunt Cuney, where she wakes up with bruises and marks on her body, it is also this sickness on board of the boat that marks the beginning of a journey towards herself. It is foremost the needs of her body that initiate Avey's self-awareness. Waxman draws the conclusion that Avey has a childlike sensitivity and vulnerability. (Waxman, *Hearth* 126) This reference to childhood is mentioned several times, but the comparison with birth and childhood denotes foremost a state of indecisiveness and insecurity, which Avey experiences at the beginning of this journey to herself ("the self-crouched like a bewildered child behind the vacant, tear-filled eyes") (*Praisesong*, 172), before she faces her own aging ("He saw how far she had come since leaving the ship and the distance she had yet to go.") (*Praisesong*, 172) Similar to the dreams of her great aunt, she experiences the encounters with the old man, who enables her definition of identity in age, as physical, violent meetings ("She felt as exhausted as if she and the old man had been fighting—actually, physically fighting.") (*Praisesong*, 184) When Avey is giving into the care of two old women on the journey by small boat to the island, they remind her of people she has met in her past. Throughout the novel her memories of the past find a correlation to her experiences in the present, which link the different stages of her life. Avey's distance to her own self finds a physical expression, when she becomes violently ill. In this passage of the novel, the two old women taking care of her make her feel like a child again ("she was seven or eight years old again"). (*Praisesong*, 208) Her lack of bodily control mirror a childlike state, and the cleansing effect is welcomed by the two old women as something good and necessary ("Then: '*Bon, li bon.*' Saying it as if even this final ignominy was a good thing in their eyes.") (*Praisesong*, 208-9) Her initial feelings of relief at giving way to the nausea turn into an orgiastic, sensual experience:

> All of a sudden, before she could even grasp what was taking place, the powerful spasms were reaching deep into her. [...] Until, to her utter disbelief, there it was: the familiar irresistible pressure, followed by the clenched muscles easing, relinquishing their hold under the pressure; and then, quickly, the helpless, almost pleasurable giving way. (Praisesong, 207)

Her initial emotion of childlike vulnerability gives way to a liberating, cathartic sexual experience. Avey does not react like a child, but accepts her own aging body as part of her identity. This interpretation is supported by another passage of the text, where Avey's clumsy movements are compared to those of a small child ("slow and clumsy as a two-year-old just learning how to undress itself") (Praisesong, 152), but her body is described as having been marked by time:

> The sodden girdle came last and after stripping it away she stood for a moment gazing vacantly down at her breasts. At the stretch lines like claw marks. At the scar where the small benign tumor had been removed when she was in her forties. At the bruised-looking nipples. (Praisesong, 151-2)

Pannill also emphasizes the age-related aspect, when she compares the bathing and massage of Avey by Lebert Jopseph's daughter, the widow Rosalie Parvay, after her arrival on the island with the bathing of a corpse or a child, thus juxtaposing death with resurrection. (Pannill, 71) Rosalie Parvay and Avey have two things in common: their age and their marital status. Rosalie, however, although a little younger than Avey has accepted her cultural identity and thus her body as part of herself: "her taut little body had already achieved his pared-down, annealed, quintessential look." (Praisesong, 216) Avey's original resistance towards Rosalie's attempts to bathe her are initially linked to her suppressed feelings: "speaking out of her obsessive privacy and the helpless aversion to being touched she had come to feel over the years" (Praisesong, 219). This bathing, however, develops from a procedure applied to a child to a sensual, sexual and finally orgiastic act, which leads to a redefinition of her identity in age and overcomes the dichotomy of body and soul:

> Until finally under the vigorous kneading and pummeling, Avey Johnson became aware of a faint stinging [...]. And this warmth and the faint stinging reached up the entire length of her thighs. [...] Then, slowly, they radiated out into her loins: When, when was the last time she had felt even the slightest stirring there? [...] The warmth, the stinging sensation that was both pleasure and pain passed up through the emptiness at her center. Until finally they reached her heart. And as they encircled her heart and it responded, there was the sense of a chord being struck. All the tendons, nerves and muscles which strung her together had been struck a powerful chord, and the reverberation could be heard in the remotest corners of her body. (Praisesong, 223-4)

Avey's memories of the happy times of her marriage emphasize the bodily aspects of the relationship, in which Avey had defined the sexual act as an act of liberation:

> And the miracle which was strictly a private matter, that had only to do with her, then took place. She slipped free of it all: the bed, the narrow hallway bedroom, the house, Halsey Street, her job, Jay, the children, and the child who might come of this embrace. She gave the slip to her ordinary, everyday self. And for a long pulsing moment, she was pure self, being, the embodiment of pleasure, the child again riding the breakers at Coney Island in her father's arms, crowing in delight and terror. (Praisesong, 128)

As this example shows, the sexual connection with another describes a movement towards the self, in which the physical experience enables an expression of self. Paule Marshall, when asked about her work, has emphasized the importance of the individual and the process of defining one's identity. (Graulich, 293) In a different context, Marshall describes sexuality as a "free zone," which allows the protagonists to escape the social limitations and find a level of communication in the physical:

I think I write about sexuality, people coming together sexually, as the place, the time in our lives when we can sometimes set aside tensions and animosities and conflict that beset us, a place where, for just a short while, we come together, embrace, and sometimes truly communicate. (Graulich, 295)

At the beginning of the novel, Marshall emphasizes bodily aspects while describing Avey's friends accompanying her on the cruise. Both Thomasina Moore ("a thin-featured woman in her early seventies with a lined and hectic brow [...]: old age beginning to warp the once graceful curve of her back") (Praisesong, 18) as well as Clarice, whose overweight is linked to her worries, show their alienation to their own selves in a physical form. While Thomasina sees Avey's announcement of her departure as a rejection of their values and thus reacts with anger and aggression, Clarice shows resignation and defeat. Avey's sudden decision to leave the cruise is interpreted as an act of deceit and abandonment of their middle class and leisurely life style that was achieved by assimilation to the dominant white culture. In contrast to Thomasina and Clarice, the two old but culturally authentic women, who take care of Avey on the passage to Carriacou, are described despite their age as physically strong and capable ("one stout and solid, the other lean, almost fleshless but with a wiry strength") (Praisesong, 205):

[...] a stout woman in her eighties with large capable hands and a gold-rimmed smile, and her thinner neighbor of the same age or older [...]. The face she turned to Avey Johnson was simply bone and a lined yellowish sheeting of skin. Old people who have the essentials to go on forever. (Praisesong, 194)

In contrast to the these women, who live in accordance with their cultural values and thus can identify with their lives, Thomasina, Clarice, and Avey are physically weakened and marked due to the alienation to their selves. This leads to both a rejection of individual as well as group identity ("it...don't... pay...to...go...no...place...with...

niggers!") (Praisesong, 28) This denial of their identity and their refusal to accept the self in the matrix of race, class, gender, and age are linked to an alienation of self and consciousness. While contemplating her past, Avey realizes that the first step towards her loss of cultural identity was the moment she started observing her own body from an outside perspective and comparing it to defined social values. When due to her pregnancy Avey no longer finds her body attractive, she loses her confidence in her identity. This socially initiated opposition to her own body leads to an alienation from her own self and in consequence from her husband Jay ("Who—*who*—was this untidy swollen woman with the murderous look?") (Praisesong, 100) As she rejects her own female form, she envisions her husband having an affair with a woman with an androgen body. She imagines her husband having a sexual affair with slim women (*"the woman's stomach was flat, smooth, a snow-white plain"*) (Praisesong, 100) and compares this with an act of birth:

Her own legs in the next three or four weeks would find themselves in the same position: raised, bent, open wide. But it would not be that lovely flowering gesture of arousal and invitation. Nor would her cries be those of ecstasy. (Praisesong, 101)

These fantasies lead to violent fights between Avey and her husband, who reacts to the unjustified reproaches by giving up the sensual and enjoyable acts they shared, such as dancing and music, in order to achieve success and wealth and determined his life strictly by rigid and passionless rules ("a harsh and joyless ethic") (Praisesong, 131). This leads to a loss of their cultural identity, as they are no longer able to link their African heritage to their American present. ("Would it have been possible to have done both?") (Praisesong, 139) Having given up the cultural values of their community and merely being motivated by a drive for material success and social mobility, their sexual acts no longer guarantee a self-confident affirmation of self, but are seen as a burden. Instead of sexual satisfaction and a feeling of connectedness after their sexual encounters, Avey experiences her loneliness even stronger ("her body left abandoned") (Praisesong,129), while her husband's longings and desire are linked to a feeling of bondage evoking associations of slavery:

And at the end his wrenching cry, "Take it from me, Avey! Just take it from me!" Love like a burden he wanted rid of. Like a leg-iron which slowed him in the course he had set for himself. (Praisesong, 129)

An important aspect in order for Avey to accept the different components of her identity in the matrix of race, class, gender, and age, involves the confrontation with her dead husband and her assessment of her married life from the distancing, clarifying perspective of widowhood. (Waxman, Widow's Journey, 96) Jay/Jerome comes to her in a dream to berate her for wasting so much money by leaving the cruise ship. His return to her in this dream triggers in Avey a host of memories that help her relive their shared lives. Her husband Jay changed his name to Jerome, when he started becoming a successful businessman and gave up due to racial and economic pressures the struggle to maintain an individual identity within their cultural community. While contemplating the early years of her marriage, Avey realizes what they both lost in the process of assimilation. Although she longingly remembers the happy times of the early years of their marriage, Avey feels guilty about these memories and they are described as deceit, sin, and addiction. It is, however, a longing she needs to give in to, as it is part of the process of self-purification and the beginning of her return to herself and her heritage: "the memories of that earlier period were a wine she could not resist" (Praisesong, 122). Avey finally mourns the loss of the warm, earthy, passionate Jay, who, she realizes had died long before the ambitious, cold Jerome. Avey can connect to the joyful, energized sex life they had, "remembrances of sex past." Waxman in her article on the importance of Avey's status as widow emphasizes the aspect of self, when she speaks of the fact that Avey's essential self, providing an exciting means of self-fulfillment is in contrast to the arrival self that Avey develops as a wife of the successful Jerome.

> This pure self markedly contrasts with the cluttered self of the older, proper, middle-class suburban matron, just as her former sensuous pleasure seems alien to the reserved, puritanical widow Avey. (Waxman, "The Widow's Journey," 96)

Only after recognizing her own involvement and guilt at having given up so easily their cultural alliances, can Avey mourn her husband, whom she lost long before his death to false dreams of assimilation and success: "Avey Johnson mourned—not his death so much, but his life." (Praisesong, 134) The recognition that she did make use of the opportunities that were offered and that they wasted their lives in the pursuit of false dreams, make her feel old: "It was bad enough to feel in her bones the old woman she had become hobbling off to her grave." (Praisesong, 143) Once on the island, after Avey has been bathed and nursed back to health by Lebert Joseph's daughter, Rosalie Parvay, Avey takes part in the ritual of the out-islanders, but at first as a passive observer, then hesitantly and carefully ("she found herself walking amid the elderly folk on the periphery") (Praisesong, 247) she begins to join the celebration (the "Big Drum"), witnessing and finally joining the important "Beg Pardon" and the dances. This section brings the novel full circle as Avey experiences reconciliation with her past, her heritage, and most importantly with her own self and thus all stages of her life reconciling not only past and present, but making it possible for her to envision a future. In her youth, Avey defined her identity and self-value merely in her conventional attractiveness and could only accept her body, when meeting a conventional norm of beauty, which very soon was called into question by her pregnancy. While Avey and her husband still lived according to their cultural roots, as soon as she returned home from work, she took off her high-heeled shoes and did her housework bare-footed. While Avey's appearances expressed at the beginning of her marriage her sexuality ("with her 1940s upsweeps and pompadours and vampish high-heeled shoes") (Praisesong, 11), later she expressed their social status of wealth and success also in her appearance by dressing according to her age and her status ("Everything in good taste and appropriate to her age.") (Praisesong, 48)

During the ritual dance on the island Avey can integrate the different perceptions of her physicality and dances in shoes with low heels ("the broad heels of her low-heeled shoes rose slightly"). (Praisesong, 248) This dance not only connects her to the suppressed and forgotten past, but offers her a perspective of the future, which reconciles the different worlds she has lived in. This is only possible by consciously accepting her own aging ("She had finally after all these decades made it across.") (Praisesong, 248) Similar to the fact that her bathing is compared to the bathing of a child, but then leads to a sensual act that offers physical satisfaction, this new beginning is compared to birth and childhood, but is very clearly connected to age and aging:

Now suddenly, as if she were that girl again, with her entire life yet to live, she felt the threads streaming out from the old people around her [...]. And their brightness as they entered her spoke of possibilities and becoming even in the face of the bare bones and the burnt-out ends. (Praisesong, 249)

This connection with others allows Avey to rediscover her own body and to feel her own self anew, which she believed to have lost over the years. While during the bathing the orgiastic emotions are evoked by the touch of another person, Rosalie Parvay, it is now Avey herself who can make these feelings happen through her own movements and the dancing leads to a physical wellbeing:

And the movement in her hips flowed upward, so that her entire torso was soon swaying. [...] All of her moving suddenly with vigor and passion she hadn't felt in years, and with something of the stylishness and sass she had once been known for. (Praisesong, 249)

She is now driven by the thought to hand on this consciousness in order to overcome what Barbara Frey Waxman has called the "mind-body fragmentation." (Waxman, *Hearth*, 121) She wants to initiate in others, what she lacked, in order to preserve her identity: consciousness, protection, memory, and distance. (Praisesong, 139) At the end of the novel, Avey decides to renovate the house she inherited from her great aunt or to build a new house there and sell the house, which is the symbol of her upward mobility. Each summer she will invite her grandchildren and the students of her youngest daughter Marion, who have the reputation of being difficult, to spend the summer there with her, and tyrannically like her great aunt she will make sure that her demands are met. At least twice a week like her great aunt did, she will lead the children to the landing place of her ancestors and tell them the story of their past. While Avey in the past found her "pure self" in the sexual connection to her husband, now in her age it is the acceptance of her own physicality, embedded in a cultural community, the spiritual link to her ancestors as well as the new won understanding to tell the children of their cultural roots, which make up their identities. Her "free-agent" status (Waxman, Widow's Journey, 97) as a widow allows this approach.

Among many other things, the novel *Praisesong for a Widow* focuses on a middle-aged woman coming to terms with her life thus far, and making a radical change in direction for the rest of her life. The need for this change is manifest in physical symptoms as well as Avey's dreams and anxieties. It is, however, only through a journey that a re-evaluation of her past and a reclaiming of her present is possible. This narrative of movement enables an existential expression of the experience of time and place by presenting Avey "journeying through duality."

Traditionally, American literary texts have used cultural representations of movement through space to talk about movement through time. In the discussed texts, travel takes on different forms, and being a tourist is often a starting point for radical changes. Identity is established in these texts by dissociation of the individuals from the known, inhibiting family ties, familiar notions about oneself and other. Only by (un)comfortably moving out of the comfort zones and by accepting life as travel, can these protagonists realize their identity-in-flux. These stories can thus be read as subversive statements of traditional concept.

Bibliography

Bauman, Zygmunt. "From Pilgrim to Tourist: Or a Short History of Identity." in *Questions of Cultural Identity*. Ed. Stuart Hall and Paul du Gay. London: Sage, 1996. 18-36. Print.

Baym, Nina. *Woman's Fiction: A Guide to Novels by and about Women in America, 1820-1870*. Ithaca: Cornell UP, 1978. Print.

Flusser, Vilém. "Exil und Kreativität." *Spuren in Kunst und Gesellschaft* 9 (Dezember/Januar1984/85): 5-9.

Graulich, Melody, Sisco, Lisa. "Meditations on Language and the Self: A Conversation with Paule Marshall." *NWSA Journal* 4.3 (Fall 1992): 282-302.

Luedtke, Luther S. Ed. *Making America. The Society & Culture of the United States*. Chapel Hill: U of North Carolina P, 1992. Print.

Mandel, Dena. "Keeping Up With Faith: Grace Paley's Sturdy American Jewess." *Studies in American Jewish Literature* 3 (1983): 85-98.

Paley, Grace. *Enormous Changes at the Last Minute*. New York: Farrar, Straus and Giroux, 1974. Print.

Pannill, Linda. "From the *Wordshop*: The Fiction of Paule Marshall." *MELUS* 12.2 (Summer1985): 63-73.

Pearson, Carol, Pope Katherine. *The Female Hero in American and British Literature*. NewYork: Bowker, 1981. Print.

Reyes, Angelita. "Politics and Metaphors of Materialism in Paule Marshall's *Praisesong forthe Widow* and Toni Morrison's *Tar Baby*." *Politics and the Muse: Studies in the Politics of Recent American Literature*. Ed. Adam J. Sorkin. Bowling Green: State U Popular Press, 1989. Print.

Taylor, Jacqueline. "Tracing Connections between Women's Personal Narrative and the Short Story of Grace Paley." *Text and Performance Quarterly* 10.1 (January 1990), p. 20-33.

Tocqueville, Alexander de. *Democracy in America*. Vol. II. 1840. New York: Knopf, 1966. Print.

Todd, Janet. *Women Writers Talking*. New York: Holmes & Meier, 1983. Print.

Waxman, Barbara Frey. *From the Hearth to the Open Road. A Feminist Study of Aging in Contemporary Literature*. New York: Greenwood, 1990. Print.

Waxman, Barbara Frey. "The Widow's Journey to Self and Roots: Aging and Society in Paule Marshall's *Praisesong for the Widow*." *Frontiers* 9.3 (1987): 94-9.

Wilentz, Gay. "Towards a Spiritual Middle Passage Back: Paule Marshall's DiasporicVision in *Praisesong for the Widow*." *Obsidian II*. 5.3 (Winter 1990): 1-21.

Woodward, Kathleen. *Figuring Age. Women, Bodies, Generations*. Bloomington: Indiana UP, 1999. Print.

Senior Tourism and Accessibility

Evolving trends and implications for the travel and tourism industry

Valeria Minghetti

INTRODUCTION

At world level, and particularly in Europe, senior population has recorded a steady growth in the last 10-15 years (UN, 2015b). The fall of birth rates coupled with an increase in life expectancy are acknowledged as the main determinants of this evolution. The main issue is to assess whether and to what extent longer life translates into an improvement of general physical and mental conditions. Most people in their 60-70s are currently more active than their peers of 20-30 years ago and can be able to do the same activities that were previously reserved to people in their 40s-50s (e.g. participate in a working activity, practice sports) (HSBC, 2009).

This aspect also relates to the subjective age of Seniors, i.e. their self perception in terms of reference age group (Le Serre, 2010). Research have shown that self image influences consumer behavior and choices and has implications for product and marketing strategies, also in tourism (Sirgy, 1982; Le Serre, 2010).

From this perspective, aging is the product of objective and subjective factors. The weight these factors have for each individual directly affects his/her physical and psychological ability and then his/her possibility to have access, on an equal basis with others, to the physical environment and to specific services.

In tourism, accessibility issues concern the whole tourist's decision-making process: from information collection and selection of the holiday destination, to booking and organization of travel, accommodation and other services; from the stay at the destination and the choice of activities to do, to the post holiday phase.

Consequently, it is a requirement that impacts the whole tourism value chain (information, transport, infrastructure and services) (Fig. 3). Ensuring equal and easy access to senior consumers and, more generally, to people with special abilities (temporary or permanent) is crucial for modern tourism businesses and destinations, in order to fulfill their physical, functional and social requirements.

The article analyses all these aspects and discusses how technology innovation can significantly contribute to reducing information barriers and to ensure social inclusion.

In detail, starting from an overview of the various definitions of "seniors", the evolution of senior population and the links among aging, disability and accessibility (Section 2), Section 3 gives an estimate of the potential accessible tourism market and describes the characteristics of the main senior market segments. Section 4 focuses the attention on how accessibility affects the whole tourism value chain and, particularly, on the role Information and Communication Technologies (ICTs) can have in facilitating the adoption of an inclusive approach. Concluding remarks research are the object of Section 5.

THE SENIORS: DEFINITIONS AND EVOLUTIONARY TRENDS

Who is the senior consumer?
Various definitions for the same concept

The review of international academic and practitioner literature highlights the lack of consensus on a proper and unique definition of "Seniors" (Alén, Dominguez and Losada, 2012; Le Serre, 2008). In marketing, two main criteria are used: the "chronological age threshold" and "retirement" (Tamaro-Hans, 1999 in Le Serre, 2008).

Regarding the first criterion, it presents some limits since the age used varies greatly among authors. According to Alén, Dominguez and Losada (2012), in the tourism domain four main approaches can be identified: those that define senior tourists as individuals aged 50 and over (e.g. Wang, 2006; Cleaver, 2000); those for whom the age threshold is 55 and over (e.g. Shim, Gehrt and Siek, 2005; Hossain, Bailey and Lubulwa, 2003) or 60 and over (e.g. Lee and Tideswell, 2005; Horneman et al., 2002); finally, those for which senior tourists are people aged 65 and over (Zimmer, Brailey and Searle, 1995). Also the European Commission and the United Nations use different thresholds for the purpose of statistics collection. The EC defines "Seniors" as people aged 55 and over (EC—DG Enterprise and Industry, 2014); the UN identifies the "older population" as formed by people aged 60 and over (UN, 2015b). These differences generally depend on the industry and the cultural context and are linked to the socio-demographic changes of society. In developed economies, the recent general improvement of health conditions and the diffusion of advanced maternal/paternal age (in the 35s-40s) tend to move the threshold forward.

As for the retirement criterion, its timing also varies from one country to another and according to social and political reformations, and can be defined using various expressions (retirement, pre-retirement age, etc.) (Le Serre, 2008).

Other authors opt for a more comprehensive definition which focuses on the qualitative transformation generated by the passing of time (LeSerre, 2008). According to this new perspective, Seniors are people who are experiencing signs of biological, psychological and/or social aging and this evolution generally affects their consumption behavior. This also taking into account that, as shown below, a senior consumer usually feels younger than his/her chronological age.

The evolution of senior population

Given the issues discussed in the previous section, the first step is to identify the size of the potential senior market. Taking the 65s as a reasonable threshold[1], the world population over 65 has shown a steady growth from 2000 onward, and this growth is expected to continue in the near future (UN, 2015a). In 2000, it accounted for about 7% of the total population and should reach a share of 11.7% at the end of 2030 (995 million) (Fig. 1).

Figure 1: Share of population over 65 on total population: past trends and forecasts to 2030 (% values)

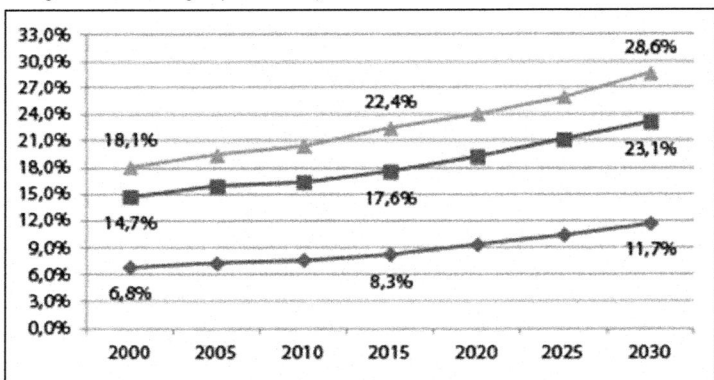

Source: author's elaborations on UN, 2015a

This trend has been pushed especially by industrial Western countries. In Italy, for example, the share of senior population was 18.1% in 2000 and should reach 28.6% in 2030 (Fig. 1). In Europe, the share is lower than in Italy (14.7% in 2000, with a projection of

---

1 | In spite of the need for a more stable concept, the statistics currently available are generally based on the chronological age threshold.

23.1% in 2030), because new member states (Eastern Europe) have a younger population than in the rest of the continent.

The fall of fertility rates in high developed countries and the improvement of life expectancy, especially in advanced age, are the main reasons for such evolution with a reduction of the gap between males and females. According to the UN, the average life expectancy of the world population will grow from 70.5 years in the period 2010-2015 to 71.7 in 2015-2020 and to 73.7 in 2025-2030, considering medium fertility evolution (UN, 2015b). In Italy, the population has recorded an average age of 82.8 years in 2010-2015 and should reach 83.8 years in 2015-20 and 85.3 years in 2025-2030.

The critical issue is whether a growing life expectancy corresponds to an "active and healthy aging" (WHO, 2002) or whether senior people simply lengthen the "limbo" period from active condition to the end of their lives. This affects the rise of first signs of physical and psychological decline and then of (temporary or permanent) difficulties and disability.

A number of analyses carried out at international level highlight a varied scenario, both among countries and within the same country, but with a clear trend towards the first option, i.e. a longer and healthier life. For example, according to the HSBC Report (2009), at world level only 16% of people aged 70 and over defined themselves in bad health (8% in mature economies). In Italy, about 16.7% of people aged between 65 and 74 stated to be in bad health in 2012, against 21.6% aged 75 and over (ISTAT, 2013). Differences arise if we distinguish between physical and psychological health: as the age progresses, the psychological status tends to be better than the physical one, especially for people aged 75 and over (ISTAT, 2013).

Age perception, disability and accessibility

High physical and mental wellbeing directly affects Seniors' perception of their age and then individual consumption behavior, also in tourism. In particular, Le Serre highlights that four non-chronological age variables (the ideal age, the cognitive age, the youth age and the discrepancy age) have important implications for understanding senior travelers' motivations, consumption behavior (e.g. destination chosen, travel organization and reservation channel used) and risk perception (Le Serre, 2010).

The *ideal age* is the age a person wishes to have, and is linked to the ideal self perception of the individual (Sirgy, 1982). The *cognitive age* refers to the age the individual identifies with, whatever his/her chronological age, and is one of the most frequently investigated variables by researchers on senior consumption behavior (see, for example, Gonzales et al., 2009). The *youth age* measures the difference between the actual and the cognitive age, i.e. the number of years a person perceives him/herself younger or older than his/her chronological age (Barak and Gould, 1985). Finally, the *discrepancy age* measures the gap between the individual's actual and ideal self-concept (the cognitive age and the ideal age) (Barak and Gould, 1985).

The investigation carried out by Le Serre in France highlights that the discrepancy age impacts on travel motivations and on physical and psychological risks' perception (i.e. the fact that holiday might not reflect the traveler's personality), the ideal age on relaxation travel motivation and on the time and psychological travel perceived risks, while the cognitive age only affects the time and psychological travel perceived risks (Le Serre, 2010). As for the youth age, it has a significant influence on intellectual travel motivations ("increase my knowledge" and "discover new places and things") (Le Serre, 2010).

Given this analysis, aging is the product of biological and psychological transformations, but also of how each individual lives them and the passing of time. The different impacts these aspects have for Seniors directly affects their ability to have access, on an equal basis with others, to the physical environment and to specific services (Fig. 2).

Figure 2: Relationship among aging, disability and accessibility

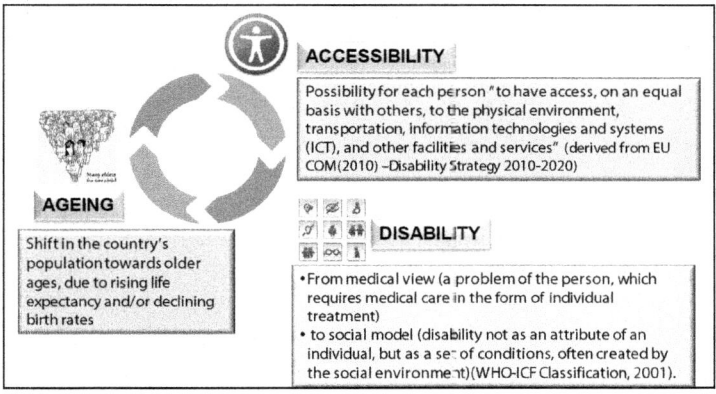

Source: author's own contribution on various sources

Regarding disability, in the last 15 years there has been a paradigm shift in the definition given by the World Health Organization (WHO, 2001). According to this new perspective, disability is no more a specific "problem of the person" (medical view), but "a set of conditions often created by the social environment" in which the person lives, that tend to discriminate him/her (social view) (Darcy and Buhalis, 2011).

In addition, there are different typologies of disabilities, which can be distinguished according to two main criteria (Minghetti and Mingotto, 2013):

- the *origin of disability*, expressed with a 'strict' vs. a 'broad' meaning: e.g. people having physical/mental impairments or a chronic disease vs. people having a potential limitation due to age or a particular situation (e.g. pregnant women, intolerant persons);
- the *duration of disability*, i.e. as a permanent or temporary condition: e.g. birth or chronic impairment vs. temporary disability caused by a particular situation and characterized by remission in a specific time span (e.g. a person with a broken bone).

These distinctions have important implications also for tourism. Figure 3 highlights, for each demand segment, the typology and intensity of their tourism requirements. The elderly population represents the largest market and, unless the presence of specific diseases or impairments, it has a moderate or low level of special needs.

Being aware of their differences is important for the tourism business and destinations in order to develop suitable product and marketing strategies (Darcy and Buhalis, 2011). In particular, the analysis of different "special" populations helps to determine:

- the size of the potential accessible tourism market and of different segments: it is reasonable to think that the number of people with generic special needs is higher than that of disabled people, and also their propensity to have a tourism experience;
- the specific requirements of accessible tourists, which are related to the type of impairment suffered, and then to the different target segments to satisfy;
- the typology of structure and services involved (hotels and other accommodation establishments, transports, information offices, attractions, etc.).

Figure 3: Pyramid of demand types: the continuum of disabilities and accessibility needs

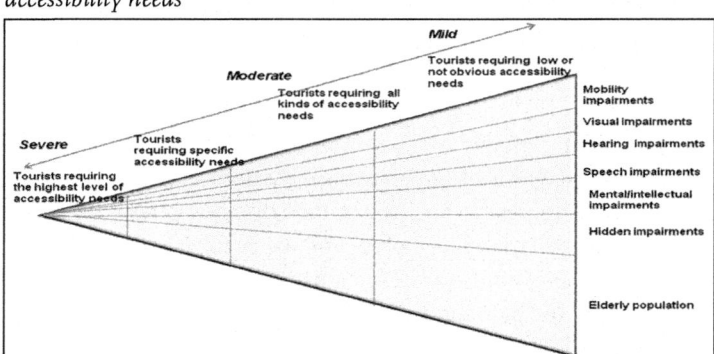

Source: Darcy and Buhalis, 2011

However, developing a "tourism for all" approach does not mean creating special products and services, but ensuring equal access to tourism facilities to all people[2], also those having special needs, no matter which difficulty they have: from disabled from birth to elderly people, from family with children to intolerant or overweight persons, etc. (Mueller, 2010).

From this point of view, accessibility is seen as both an ethic and a commercial opportunity. At destination level, not only a wider usability of the tourism system is an advantage for senior and "special" tourists, but also for elderly people and disabled residents in the area (Alén, Dominguez and Losada, 2012).

SENIOR TOURISM VS. ACCESSIBLE TOURISM: MAIN ISSUES

The size of the potential accessible tourism market

From what discussed just above, senior tourism and accessible tourism are not synonymous. Elderly people may not have any special need, or may not reveal it, in comparison to the rest of the tourism market. On the other hand, young or adult tourists with physical or mental impairments can require specific accessible services. Consequently, senior and disabled tourism populations are only partially overlapping. But how many people with special needs are potentially interested in traveling? The following table provides, for Europe and Italy, an estimate of the size of the senior population, of the disabled population, and of the total potential accessible tourist market, also including accompanying persons (e.g. relatives and friends).

---

2 | This is the philosophy behind the Universal Design approach, which aims at creating an environment without barriers, where every person can access and enjoy different products and services, taking into account the continuum of human abilities/disabilities described just above and their variability over time (Center for Universal Design, 1997).

According to UN data, in 2012 EU population aged 65 and over amounted to 123.6 mln (16.8% of total EU population). In Italy, 12,6 million individuals were over 65 (21.2% of total population) (Tab. 1).

*Table 1: Senior tourism vs. accessible tourism:
the size of the potential market*

	Population aged 65 and over in 2012 (UN, 2015a)	Disabled people in 2012 (Grammenos, 2014)	Size of the potential accessible tourist market in 2012
EUROPE	123.6 mln (16.8% of total population)	155.7 mln over 16 (severe and moderate disability) (26.1% of total population aged 16 and over)	• 64.6 mln tourists (57.6% people over 65 and 42.4% disabled aged 15-64) (1) • 97 mln if also accompanying persons are included
ITALY	12.6 mln (21.2% of total population)-	14.4 mln over 16 (severe and moderate disability) (29.2% of total population aged 16 and over)	• 5.5-6.3 mln tourists (2) • 7.5-8.6 mln if accompanying persons included

Source: author's elaborations on various sources
Note: (1) GfK et al., 2014; (2) CISET elaborations on Eurostat, Bank of Italy and ISTAT data

As for the disabled population, the EU-SILC survey[3] indicates that in 2012 26% of the total EU population aged 16 and over presented moderate or severe disabilities (Grammenos, 2014). In Italy the share was 29.2%. If we apply these percentages to UN data, this would mean about 155.7 million individuals in Europe and 14.4 mil-

---

3 | The EU-SILC survey defines "people with disabilities" as "persons limited in activities people usually do, because of health problems, for at least the last 6 months" (Grammenos, 2014: 4). It covers all individuals with these characteristics, aged 16 years old and over and living in private households.

lion in Italy. Taking into account that disability increases with age and that 54.5% of the EU senior population aged 65 and over declares limitations in activities (Grammenos, 2014), this would mean about 67.4 million seniors, representing about 43.3% of total EU disabled population aged 16 and over. In Italy, the share of disabled seniors is higher (62.8% of total population aged 65 and over, equal to 7.9 mln), weighting for about 55% of total Italian disabled population aged 16 and over.

Another study developed by GfK (Gfk et al., 2014) estimates that in 2012 Europeans with special needs (including both elderly and disabled people) were about 138.6 million, of which 36% of disabled people aged 15-64 (49.9 million) and 64% of elderly people (aged 65 and over: 88.7 million). On average, about 55% of the individuals with disabilities show a propensity to travel (27.4 million), in comparison to 42% of elderly people during the same period (37.2 million). This means a total of 64,6 mln potential travelers (Tab.2). Considering that usually people with special needs travel with accompanying persons and taking a multiplier effect of 1.5 (i.e. 1 accessible tourist out of 2 travel with another person), this means a total potentially accessible tourism population of about 97 million people in the European Union.

As for Italy, the estimates made by CISET—and based on EU-SILC, Bank of Italy and ISTAT data—indicates a potential domestic tourism market (disabled and elderly people) of about 4.1-4.9 million people aged 16 and above, which would rise to 5.7-6.8 million if also accompanying persons were included (Minghetti and Mingotto, 2014). Tourists arriving from EU countries are about 1.4 million (1.8 million if also accompanying persons are included). This equates to a total potential accessible tourism market of 5.5-6.3 million tourists (7.5-8.6 million, if accompanying persons are also included).

Analyzing the tourism behavior of Europeans with special needs, in 2012 they generated about 781 million travels, of which 395 million were same-day-excursions (51%) and 386 million were overnight holidays (at least 1 night: 49%) (GfK et al., 2014) (Tab. 2).

Table 2: Tourism behavior of people with special needs (elderly and disabled people), according to travel type. EU27 average. 2012

	Elderly people (65 and over)		Disabled people (15-64)	
	Daily excursion	Holiday (1 night or more)	Daily excursion	Holiday (1 night or more)
Total travels (mln)	225	217	170	169
Travel propensity on total population	36.4%	47.5%	51.8%	58.1%
Travel frequency (average no. of trips)	7.0	5.1	6.6	5.8
Destination: · Domestic (%) · EU (%) · Extra Europe (%)	87.3% 12.1% 0.6%	70.0% 22.8% 7.2%	87.1% 10.4% 2.5%	60.1% 27.4% 12.5%

Source: GfK et al., 2014

Elderly people, in particular, made about 442 million travels (56% of the total), of which 225 million were day-trips and 217 million were holidays (Tab. 2). About 87% of daily excursions have their country of residence as destination, while 12% choose the rest of Europe. As for holidays, 70% are spent in their home country, while 22.8% in other European destinations. On average, according to this analysis, senior tourists make almost seven daily excursions and five holidays with at least one night away from home during a year. The corresponding data for disabled people are shown in Table 2.

Senior tourism: one population, two segments

In spite of the lack of a universally accepted definition of seniors, elderly consumers have received increasing attention from the economic, marketing and social literature as well as from international institutions (United Nations, European Commission) (EU,2014). Because of their recent evolution, seniors represent a promising market also for tourism: they have disposable money and time to travel, usually take more holidays per year and stay longer at the destination (see, for example, Singh, 2014; Alén, Dominguez and Losada, 2012).

However, as a number of studies have also highlighted, they are not a homogeneous group. This because people of the same age can have different lifestyles, cultures, experiences and health. All these aspects affect travel motivation, destination choice, service preferences and expected benefits (see, for example, Ward, 2014).

Focusing on the segmentation of the senior tourism market, if we consider the two variables discussed in the previous section, disability and accessibility, two broad categories of tourists can be defined:

- the "grey" or "silver" tourists: adults with some old age sign but still active and in good health, often retired and usually with an extensive experience in tourism. Marketing studies define them using different definitions (e.g. GRAMPIES-Growing Retired Active Moneyed People in Excellent State, YOLLIES—Young Old Leisured people) (van der Steina, 2014). They are demanding consumers and have a significant economic market potential. They are used to travel away from peak seasons, sometimes also with grandchildren. In case they have some minor impairment or special needs, they generally prefer to hide them, in order not to be treated differently from other tourists;
- the "special need" tourists: people with health problems (e.g. chronic diseases) or limitations in activities, but still eager to travel and enjoy a holiday away from home. For them accessibility and mobility are core issues (transports, accommodation, etc.),

as well as the presence of medical assistance at the destination. They generally travel with accompanying person(s) and require specific services and assistive devices.

The share of "grey" tourists on the total senior tourism market is generally higher, because the perception of poor accessibility and the lack of adequate information on available facilities and services is often a deterrent for potential "special need" tourists to travel.

Promoting "Tourism for All": The Role of ICTs in a Universal Design Approach

Accessibility and the tourism value chain: modeling tourist services for different level of abilities/disabilities

In general, the wishes and expectations of elderly tourists and, more generally, of tourists with special needs do not differ materially from those of able-bodied persons.

Four main pillars summarize the basic requirements placed on an accessible holiday (FMET, 1994) (Fig. 4). "Information" means easy access to all important information when planning and taking the holiday (simplicity, variety, clarity, etc.). A recent survey carried out on a sample of the senior EU tourist population aged 55 and over (AGE Platform Europe, 2015) shows that easy access to information and services has great value for these tourists: 52.3% rank it very important and 32.3% important, with higher percentages for tourists aged 65 and over.

"Service" relates to the recognition of senior tourists and, more generally, of tourists with special needs, as a target group in its own right (friendly and easy interaction; competent, qualified contact persons; customized solutions and assistance). According to the same survey, beyond information regarding tourism facilities, those on the presence of health care and medical services have a great importance for senior tourists (55% rank them as very important, 26,2% as important) (AGE Platform Europe, 2015).

Figure 4: Main pillars of an accessible holiday for all

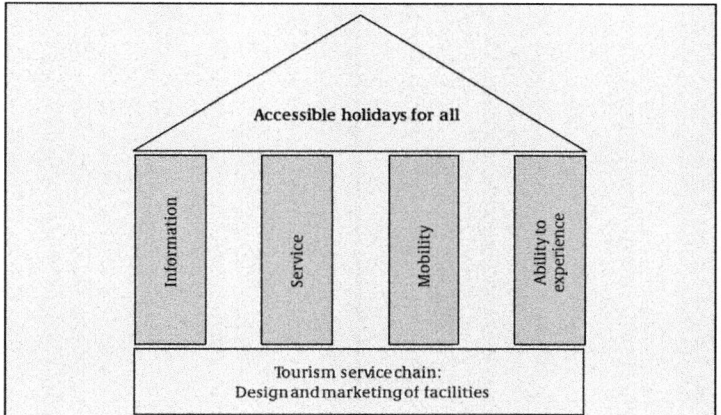

Source: FMET-Federal Ministry of Economics and Technology of Germany (1994)

"Mobility" concerns the possibility to move around the destination independently (i.e. accessibility to infrastructure and transports, tourism facilities and attractions; ability to move around these facilities and attractions). Finally, "Ability to experience" means the possibility to enjoy a range of different tourism services at the holiday destination (i.e. accessible accommodation and dining establishments; accessible tourist sites and resorts; accessible cultural and leisure facilities and services) (Fig. 4).

Consequently, accessibility affects the whole tourist decision-making process: from information collection and choice of the destination, to travel and holiday booking and organization, to the stay at the destination, and to post holiday. This means that the whole tourism value chain is involved in providing user-friendly information, products and services (Fig. 5).

Figure 5: The "accessible" tourism value chain

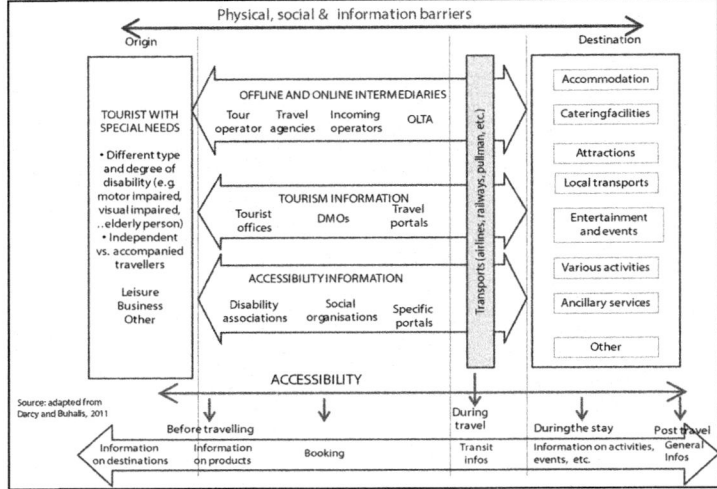

Source: author's elaboration on Eichhorn and Buhalis, 2011

Focusing on information accessibility, in the first steps of the decision-making process (before traveling), information on destinations, local products and services, and on booking systems play a crucial role for tourists with special needs planning a holiday. During the travel and the stay, information on physical and temporal accessibility to infrastructures and local activities and services (transport, cultural and leisure services, etc.) rank first. This information is crucial for tourists to check their ability to have a fulfilling tourism experience at destination. Accessibility maintains its importance also in the post holiday phase, when tourists with special needs may wish to share their positive or negative experience with others (Fig. 5).

As concerns the role of tourism operators, potential customers with different requirements and information needs represent an important opportunity and challenge for the travel and tourism industry (Darcy and Buhalis, 2012). If tourists with the highest accessibility requirements can be better served by specialized tourism operators, who have profound knowledge of their needs, tourists with moderate or mild requirements, such as 'grey' tourists, can use products and services offered by the majority of tourism operators, especially of those who have adopted an inclusive approach. This because these people "do not feel that they should be using specialized facilities that may stigmatize them" (Darcy e Buhalis, 2011).

Towards an accessible tourism information system: main challenges

Information and Communication Technologies (ICTs) can play a crucial role in facilitating the realization of a "tourism for all" approach. The development and implementation of digital tools, platforms and applications can help to reduce physical and information barriers, enabling both disabled and elderly people to better integrate into society (Michopolou and Buhalis, 2011).

Regarding elderly people, they are often considered as "technology anxious and reluctant to adopt new technologies" (Pesonen, Komppula and Riihinen, 2015: 832). However, in spite of their still modest level of adoption, seniors are the most dynamic group of internet users and online information seekers, and the percentage of individuals with good ICT skills tends to increase over time. According to Eurostat, in 2014 about 42% of EU citizens aged 65 and over have used the internet in the last 3 months, against 38% in 2013 and 34% in 2012 (+11.7% on average each year). The percentages are, respectively, 78%, 75% and 73% if we consider the total EU population (+3.4% on average each year) (Eurostat, 2015).

Anyway, websites, platforms and applications are not easily accessible to everyone. ICTs have to be designed to accommodate the needs of all users, thus ensuring general accessibility and usability, regardless of the degree of disablement. Assistive technologies can help people to interact with ICTs, "providing a wide range of input and output devices, such as specialized keyboards and screen readers" (Michopolou and Buhalis, 2011: 297).

Focusing on information barriers, an accessible tourism information system should be designed to fulfill the content and technical requirements of tourists with special needs, having different type and degree of disability and travelling alone or with accompanying persons, for different purposes. The planning of such a system requires that four key issues have been addressed: interoperability; content integration; personalization; and accessible design (Fig. 6).

The first three issues are important for the whole tourism system, while the last one, accessible design, is critical for those using assistive technologies. *Interoperability* describes "the extent to which systems and devices can exchange data, and interpret that shared data"[4]. Tourism in its nature is an industry strongly dependent on information exchange, but the heterogeneity of data sources requires standardization guidelines. This in order to promote the co-operation among the various operators involved, ensure that tourists receive the information required and then create an accessibility path.

Figure 6: Information e-accessibility and usability: key issues

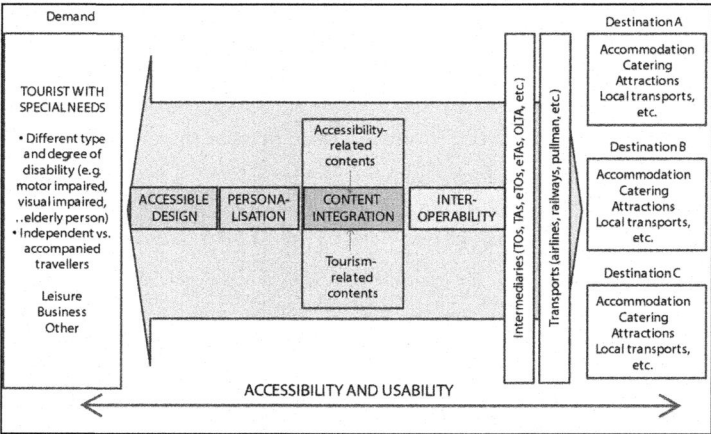

Source: author's elaboration on Michopolou and Buhalis, 2011

---

4 | HIMSS definition (http://www.himss.org/library/interoperability-standards/what-is-interoperability)

As regards *content integration*, information is critical for travelers with limitations (Michopolou and Buhalis, 2012). This means to integrate general tourism information provided by destination management organizations, local authorities, travel guides, etc. with specific accessibility-related contents. A further complication is that each type of limitation/disability requires different levels of accessibility information: e.g. if 'grey' tourists and, more generally, tourists with low level of limitations requires basic accessibility information, their specificity grows as the degree of disablement increases.

From this point of view, *personalization* means filtering tourism and accessibility information according to the type and severity of limitation/disability. This in order to allow potential tourists "to choose the products and services that best serve their individual abilities and preferences by trading off with parameters such as available facilities, venue location and price" (Michopolou and Buhalis, 2012: 295).

Finally, *accessible design* is critical for those tourists using assistive technologies to navigate the internet sites. As the authors highlight, the majority of tourism websites are usually found inaccessible, mainly those targeting accessible audience.

Conclusions

> "Age is an issue of mind over matter. If you don't mind, it doesn't matter"
> (M. Twain)

Despite the lack of a universally shared definition in literature, due to the variability of the aging process (Ward, 2014) and of self-perception, seniors are acknowledged as an important market for tourism, given the increasing number of active and healthy pensioners. 'Grey' tourists are generally well experienced and differ from earlier generations of their peers in many ways, in particular for the growing use of Information and Communication Technologies as part of their information search (Pesonen, Komppula and Riihinen, 2015). But also mature tourists with declared special needs show a higher propensity to travel than some decades ago.

Physical, social and information accessibility represent key features for tourism businesses and destinations interested in attracting these tourism segments. Providing integrated and personalized tourism and accessibility-related contents, also through system interoperability and co-operation among different stakeholders, is crucial to help tourists to make an informed choice. Furthermore, the development of 'open' infrastructures and services can contribute to make them live a memorable experience at destination. Given the current evolution of society, these aspects would become pivotal for the future competitiveness of hotels, transports and other tourism-related facilities as well as for beach resorts, art cities and other tourism places.

Works Cited

AGE Platform Europe. *Report on Senior Tourists needs and demands*, ESCAPE, 2015 <http://www.ageplatform.eu/images/ESCAPE_Needs_and_expectations_FINAL.pdf>. Web.

Alén Elisa, Domìnguez Trinidad and Nieves Losada. "New Opportunities for the Tourism Market: Senior Tourism and Accessible Tourism." *Visions for Global Tourism Industry: Creating and Sustaining Competitive Strategies*. Ed. Murat Kasimoglu. In Tech Pub. 2012. 139-66. Print.

Barak B. and Gould S. "Alternative Age Measures: A Research Agenda." Eds. Hirschman E.C. and Holbrook M.B., Association for Consumer Research, 12 (1985): 53-8. <http://www.acrwebsite.org/search/view-conferenceproceedings.aspx?Id=6357 >. Web.

Center for Universal Design—"The Principles of Universal Design." 1997. <http://www.ncsu.edu/ncsu/design/cud/about_ud/udprinciplestext.htm>. Web.

Cleaver, M. "Australian seniors' use of travel information sources: perceived usefulness of word-of-mouth, professional advice, marketer-dominated and general media information." *ANZMAC 2000 Visionary Marketing for the 21 st Century*, 2000, 1-6. Print.

Darcy, Simon and Dimitrios Buhalis. "Conceptualizing Disability." *Accessible Tourism: Concepts and Issues*. Eds. Buhalis D., Darcy S. Bristol: Channel View Publications, 2011. 21-45. Print.

Eichhorn, Victoria and Dimitrios Buhalis. "Accessibility: A Key Objective for the Tourism Industry." *Accessible Tourism: Concepts and Issues*, Eds. Buhalis D., Darcy S. Bristol: Channel View Publications, 2011. 46-61. Print.

European Commission—DG Enterprise and Industry (2014), *Europe: the best destination for seniors, draft report*. Service Industry, Tourism Policy—Ref. Ares (2014)2478246-25/07/2014. Print.

Eurostat, Information Society Statistics Database, 2015 <http://ec.europa.eu/eurostat/web/information-society/data/database>. Web.

FMET—Federal Ministry of Economics and Technology of Germany, *Economic Impulses of Accessible Tourism for All. Summary of results*, 1994 <http://www.bmwi.de/English/Redaktion/Pdf/economic-impulses-of-accessible-tourism-for-all-526,property=pdf, bereich=bmwi,sprache=en,rwb=true.pdf >. Web.

GfK, University of Surrey, Neumann Consulting, Pro Solutions, *Economic Impact and travel patterns of accessible tourism in Europe*—Final Report, Study A, Service Contract SI2.ACPROCE052481700—EU, DG Enterprise and Industry, 2014 <http://ec.europa.eu/DocsRoom/documents/5566/attachments/1/.../en/.../native>. Web.

Gonzales Ana Maria, Rodrıguez Carmen, Miranda Mauro R. and Miguel Cervantes. "Cognitive age as a criterion explaining senior tourists' motivations." *International Journal of Culture, Tourism and Hospitality Research*, 3.2 (2009): 148-64. Print.

Grammenos, Stefanos. *European comparative data on Europe 2020 & People with disabilities Task 6: Comparative data and indicators*, CESEP, December 2014, on behalf of ANED, < http://www.disability-europe.net/theme/statistical-indicators>. Web.

Horneman, Louise, Carter, R. W., Wei Sherrie and Hein Ruys. "Profiling the senior traveler: An Australian perspective." *Journal of Travel Research*. 41.1 (2002): 23.

Hossain, A., Bailey, G. and M. Lubulwa. "Characteristics and Travel Patterns of Older Australians: Impact of Population Aging on Tourism". *International Conference on Population Aging and Health: Modeling our Future*, Canberra, Australia, 2003. Print.

HSBC. *The Future of Retirement. It's time to prepare*, HSBC Insurance Holding Ltd, 2009 <http://www.us.hsbc.com/1/PA_1_083Q9FJ08 A002FBP5S00000000/content/usshared/Premier/Shared/pdfs/FoR5_Report_2009.pdf >. Web.

ISTAT (2013), *La salute e il ricorso ai servizi sanitari. Dati 2012*, <http://www.istat.it/it/archivio/108565>. Web.

Lee, Sun Hee and Carmen Tideswell. "Understanding attitudes towards leisure travel and the constraints faced by senior Koreans." *Journal of Vacations Marketing*. 11.3 (2005): 249-63. Print.

Le Serre, Dominique. "Segmenting the senior tourism market: Identification of Subjective Ages' Influences on Seniors' Travel Motivations." *Proceeding of the International Marketing Trends Conference 2010*, <http://www.marketing-trends-congress.com/archives/2010/Materiali/Paper/Fr/LeSerre.pdf>. Web.

Le Serre, Dominique. "Who is the senior consumer?" *Proceedings on the International Marketing Trends Conference 2008*, <http://www.marketingtrends-congress.com/2008_cp/Materiali/Paper/Fr/LeSerre.pdf>. Web.

Michopolou, Elina and Dimitrios Buhalis. "Technology Platforms and Challenges." *Accessible Tourism: Concepts and Issues*. Eds. Buhalis D. and Darcy S. Bristol: Channel View Publications, 2011. 287-99. Print.

Minghetti, Valeria. *Veneto for All. Rilevanza economica e sociale del turismo accessibile e linee guida per lo sviluppo in Veneto*, Final Report, 2014, Veneto Regional Government (Internal document). Print.

Minghetti, Valeria and Erica Mingotto. *Veneto for All. Come garantire l'esperienza turistica per tutti e migliorare l'accoglienza e la competi-

tività di un territorio, Final Report, 2013, Veneto Regional Government (Internal document). Print.

Mueller, Lillian. "Il turismo accessibile secondo gli studi e le prassi in Europa." *Viaggiare senza limiti: il Turismo per Tutti in Europa*. Eds. Bravo N. and Manzo A., IsITT, Ottobre 2010.18-26. <http://www.cpdconsulta.it/file/lib/data/viaggiare_senza_limiti_def_pantone.pdf>. Web.

Pesonen, Juno, Komppula, Raija and Annina Riihinen. "Senior Travellers as Users of Online Travel Services: A Qualitative Enquiry." *Information and Communication Technologies in Tourism 2015*, Eds. Tussyadyah, I Inversini A. Proceedings of the ENTER International Conference in Lugano, Switzerland, February 3-6, 2015. 831-43. Print.

Peters, George R. "Self Conception of the Aged. Age Identification and Aging." *The Gerontologist*. 11 (1971): 69-73. Print.

Shim, Soyeon, Gehrt, Kenneth C. and Mai Siek. "Attitude and behavior regarding pleasure travel among mature consumers: A socialisation perspective." *Journal of Travel and Tourism Marketing*. 18.2 (2005): 69-81. Print.

Singh, Ranbir. "Senior tourism: An analysis of holiday purchase decisions and major behavioural constraints." *International Journal of Research in Economics and Social Sciences*. 4.5 (2014): 92-102. Print.

Sirgy, M. Joseph. "Self Concept in Consumer Behaviour: A Critical Review." *Journal of Consumer Research*. 9.9 (1982): 297-99. Print.

UN-United Nations, Population Division. *World Population Prospects Database. The 2015 revision*, Department of Economic and Social Affairs, 2015a <http://esa.un.org/unp d/wpp/DataQuery/>. Web.

UN-United Nations. *World Population Prospects. Key findings & advance tables. The 2015 revision*, Department of Economic and Social Affairs, 2015b <http://esa.un.org/unpd /wpp/Publications/Files/Key_Findings_WPP_2015.pdf>. Web.

Wang, Kuoc C. "Motivations for Senior Groups Package Tour Tourists." *Journal of Tourism Studies*. 12.2 (2006): 119-38. Print.

Ward, Aisling. "Segmenting the senior tourism market in Ireland based on travel motivations." *Journal of Vacation Marketing.* 20.3 (2014): 267-77. Print.

WHO-World Health Organization. *Active aging. A Policy framework,* 2002, <http://whqlibdoc.who.int/hq/2002/WHO_NMH_NPH_02.8.pdf?ua=1>. Web.

WHO-World Health Organization. *International Classification of Functioning, Disability and Health* (ICF), 2001 <http://www.who.int/classifications/icf/icf_more/en/>. Web.

Zimmer, Z., Braley, R.E. and M.S. Searle. "Whether to go and where to go: identification of important influences on senior's decisions to travel." *Journal of Travel Research.* 33 (1995): 3-10. Print.

Undermining Retirement as Leisure Time in Deborah Moggach's *These Foolish Things* and *The Best Exotic Marigold Hotel*

Maricel Oró-Piqueras

SENIOR TOURISM: AGEING AND OLD AGE WITHIN CONSUMER CULTURE

In the last decades, the changing patterns in production and consumption together with the progressive ageing of the population have turned those citizens in their sixties, seventies, eighties and beyond into potential long-term consumers of the tourist industry. According to Andrew Blaikie (1999), during the fifties and sixties retirement was characterised as "a time of crisis and sickness" which should be avoided at all costs since retirement was equated to "social death" (63). In the seventies and eighties, with the economy requiring mass employment, "retirement was reinterpreted as an active choice" (63). This is when retirement starts being perceived as a time of leisure which one could organise according to personal preferences as well as income. With consumer culture and advertising, retirement is increasingly equated to a time of leisure in which one is expected to make the most of one's time left. In that sense, Blaikie concludes that leisure, the activities with which one spends one's time after retirement, start defining those in old age. However, one of the implications of consumer culture is the fact that the images that reach the wider audience through advertisement tend to be idealised conceptions of old age as leisure time. Usually, advertisement on holidays and vacation packs directed to the senior population show imagines of athletic and dynamic citizens in their sixties and seventies. Silvering white hair, wide smiles and tanned skins characterise the retired tourists in advertising campaigns; relaxing strolls close to a paradisiacal beach or a couple looking at a colourful sunset are recurrent images attached to senior tourism.

Mike Featherstone and Hepworth (1990, 1995) analysed the extent to which images of positive ageing go hand in hand with the identification of a growing target market among the senior population. In particular, they focused on analysing a British magazine entitled *Retirement Choice Magazine*. Featherstone and Hepworth argue that a major change can be observed both in the layout and content of the magazine around mid-1970s. Whereas in the past retirement was presented as mostly a passive time in which one was expected to rest and be quite inactive, around 1972 the magazine starts introducing changes in order to call the attention of men and women in mid-life who could be attracted to "a long-term interest in leisure planning" (1990, 272). Thus, travelling and holidays is related to a new generation of retirees who, according to Featherstone and Hepworth, "see themselves and feel themselves to be far distanced from the passive and less exhilarating traditional image of middle age as the threshold of a disengaged old age" (1990, 272).

In "Creating Memories. Some Images of Aging in Mass Tourism" (1995), David Chaney analyses holidays brochures directed to British senior tourism. With the increasing number of retired citizens who leave a full-time job and can count on a fixed income and the changing traditions of family structure, with more older citizens living either with their peers or on their own, Chaney argues that "the normative expectations of aging are continually being renegotiated" so that new experiences within the ageing process are represented and finally integrated as traditional forms. This is the case of winter holidays which, especially from the 1990s onwards are "not presented as Utopian contrasts but offer affirmations of identity which deny novelty through the invention of tradition" (213).

According to Chaney, in these brochures, identity is constructed as "stages (that is, sites for performance) for a distinctive social milieu" (214) rather than as specific destinations where retired citizens will actually visit and learn from the place. These destinations are presented as not far away from English culture, with already familiar activities and with a climate similar to that of a warm English spring day; in other words, winter holidays in warmer European countries are described as part of the tradition of the culture of ageing, as Chaney defines it: "[t]he evocation of holidays is also a way of talking about the sorts of concerns that can be expected to dominate the culture of aging; and thus, in this and a thousand other discursive forms a way in which this culture is learnt and understood" (215). However, Chaney describes this discourse in 90s British brochures as "a discourse which ignores difference and claims the warrant of tradition" (215).

Researchers in senior tourism have identified an evolution in the consumers and their choices from the 1990s until the present time. With the growing number of senior citizens, tourism industry has become aware of the marketing challenges that this implies. A growing ageing population with a longer life expectancy, a more open conception of retirement as leisure time and "a growing propensity to travel and spend" (509), as pointed out by Hunter-Jones and Blackburn (2007) has had an influence on what senior tourism can offer to senior citizens. Lohmann and Danielsson (2001), Hunter-Jones and Blackburn (2007), and Patterson and Pegg (2011) define senior tourism as not being perceived as a homogeneous group any longer; on the contrary, they are seen as consumers with new interests who go on holiday in order to "escape, socialise, fantasise and be creative" (Patterson and Pegg 174) rather than recreate their native countries in a warmer place. The positive sides on the health and sociability derived from the diverse possibilities offered to the senior sector has been assessed by Hunter-Jones and Blackburn. In their article "Understanding the relationship between holiday taking and self-assessed health: an exploratory study of senior tourism", they conclude that holiday taking "offered significant benefits to respondents in terms of personal health (psychological and physical) and social effectiveness" (514). However, despite the wider range of possibilities offered to senior citizens and despite the positive outcomes of travelling and relating to people within other backgrounds and circumstances, advertising images in senior tourism still contribute to present narrowing images of old age in terms of physical appearance and keeping the signs of ageing at bay. Moreover, disability and infirmity in old age are still left out of the picture of this "golden old age". In relation to health issues, Hunter-Jones and Balckburn explain that recurring concerns were identified by respondents (such as injections, humidity, airport stress, being subjected to an insurance lottery) and highlight the need of the industry to establish a direct connection with senior tourists in order to offer a more comprehensive service.

FICTIONALISING AN EXTREME FORM OF SENIOR TOURISM

Deborah Moggach presents a double-sided reality of senior tourism in her novel *These Foolish Things* since the older characters in the novel are not only going to spend a few weeks in an exotic place, but, actually, the rest of their retirement years. *These Foolish Things* presents an extreme form of senior tourism in which the fact of moving from their native country to an exotic place with less restrictive norms gives the characters a new lease of life; but, on the other hand, spending their retirement in a foreign country also reminds the retired characters of the fact that they are a nuisance in their own country. Thus, the novel shows the positive effect that moving to another country has for older citizens, but at the same time it underscores the failure of that same society in offering plausible and creative options for an increasingly ageing population.

Deborah Moggach's *These Foolish Things* was published in 2004 and turned into a film in 2012, with the title *The Best Exotic Marigold Hotel* and some significant changes. The film was directed by John Madden, with a screenplay by Ol Parker and the cast consists of well-known actors and actresses most of whom have aged on the screen; namely, Judi Dench, Celia Imri, Bill Nighy, Ronald Picup, Maggie Smith, Tom Wilkinson and Penelope Wilton. Both, the novel and the film, are set in London at the beginning of the twenty-first century and they portray a group of old characters who decide to move to Dunroamin Retirement Hotel—The Best Exotic Marigold Hotel in the case of the film—in India, to spend their retirement years there. However, the reasons behind their decision to move to India do not respond to their wish of enjoying some time in an exotic place, but mainly to the fact that they seem not to fit in their native country. The main characters decide to move to India because they feel lonely and obliterated by both their communities and families and by the shrinking economic resources on which they can count. The main characters in the novel who also appear in the film are Evelyn Greenslade, who is left without any money once her husband dies; Muriel Donnelly, also living on her own and with an only child who is on the run from the police; Douglas and Jean Ainslie who are unable to make ends meet with their pensions; Norman, who dreams about having endless sexual experiences with attractive women; Madge, who is looking for a Maharaja, and Graham, a single retired judge who decides to go back to India to recover some of his childhood memories and come to terms with it, instead of staying in England and having a monotonous and lonely retirement[1].

From the group of British characters, there is only one couple who is described as having travelled around since their retirement. Jean and Douglas, especially Jean, define themselves as quite adventurous, "A couple of vagabonds" (82). In this case, Jean identifies travelling and holidays with economic affluence and an active

---

1 | In *These Foolish Things*, there appears another main character who is not present in the film, Dorothy Miller. She is described as a retired TV presenter who spends most of her time at home. After having been a public and admired figure for such a long time, Dorothy Miller finds it difficult to come to terms with anonymity and increasing invisibility. Thus, for her, moving to India is a new start.

and exciting retirement, as opposed to those citizens who equate retirement to inactivity. Jean is projecting a specific image of herself and her husband which would match the image present in advertising campaigns directed to senior tourists; that is, healthy and active retirees who spend their time and money exploring the world and relaxing themselves. This image would be the exact opposite of a deprived old age, either in terms of economic resources or health, or both, and which would be considered as unsuccessful ageing in Western society. In this respect, despite the unquestionable advantages that senior tourism provides to retired people as described by Hunter-Jones and Balckburn, the fact of being able to travel and go on holidays is closely related to a restricted image of old age. In her *Learning to be Old. Gender, Culture and Ageing*, Margaret Cruickshank (2002) questions the idea of "successful aging" and argues that it cannot really be applied to a "complex human process" (2) such as aging in which variables such as gender, class and ethnicity are not considered. Moreover, the term "successful" focuses on the concept of effort and achievement, obliterating the element of luck which is actually one of the variables which may influence a long life.

In fact, despite Jean trying to give this image of being a fashionable, active and opulent couple, both the readers and viewers know that the decision behind Jean and Douglas to move to Dunroamin Retirement Hotel lies in the fact that their economic resources are shrinking and, thus, they decide to try to have a better old age somewhere else, a place where they could make the most of their pensions. One could argue that *These Foolish Things* and *The Best Exotic Marigold Hotel* also question the concept of successful ageing since there is little the characters who decide to move to India can do to improve their personal situations in their own country; a situation which seems to take them to loneliness and shortage of resources. In this scenario, both the novel and the film suggest that their only chance is to look for a better future in another country. Evelyn Greenslade, well-aware of the narrowing options she has left as an older widower without a fixed income and without savings observes once on the plane which is going to take her to Bangalore, India: "She knew, of course, that she had no choice. Wherever she went, this was what she had to do now. Even if she came home again, which she might, this same situation would face her" (85).

In an article published on *The Telegraph* online, Moggach considers that her portrayal of the future of an ageing British society is quite plausible since "we are all being kept alive", but more importantly, "more of us are living alone" and it means that "there isn't someone to pick them up when they fall" (1). Moggach's vision actually matches with Norbert Elias's and Haim Hazan's research in which they argue that "social death precedes biological death" (Hazan 68) in advanced complex societies. For both Elias and Hazan, old age is increasingly made invisible and separated from everyday life due to its closeness to death. According to Hazan, "the separation of the aged from society, the identification of ageing with ugliness, evil and horror and the reluctance to engage in physical contact with the aged, all indicate that ageing is perceived as a dangerous area located between life and death" (68). Moreover, he considers that the aged themselves "always identify other as older and therefore closer to death" (68). Whereas Deborah Moggach's novel presents, in a humorous way, a possible solution to the social problem of an ageing population in which old age is still not seen as an intrinsic part of all human beings and, thus, it is ignored and made invisible, it also criticises the place left to old age in Western societies. In the film, there is a very significant scene which takes place in the airport on the main characters' one-way trip to India. The flight of the protagonists is delayed and the seven main characters are sitting in a row of chairs, one beside the other, in an impeccable terminal with floors that mirror what is above them and with no one around. The terminal and its neatness, as well as the silvery colour of the floor and ceiling and the bluish reflection of the glasses of the terminal reminds the viewer of an institution such as a hospital or an old people's home. For a moment, the viewer is left with the doubt whether the final destiny of these characters is going to be the same as the one from which they are trying to escape in their own country. Few scenes later, the bustling and jostling of the

Indian city proves that they are actually escaping the narrowing options they are offered in England.

The novel actually begins when Dr. Ravi and his cousin Sonny decide to set up a retirement home in India so that those senior citizens who feel lonely, abandoned and bored can spend their last days in a place where they are not only well-cared for and respected, but where they can also enjoy the sun and the multiple possibilities on offer. When Dr Ravi and Sonny start planning their new business, it is interesting to analyse how they perceive senior tourism, in other words, how old conceptions of tourism and of old age and ageing mingle with a new generation of senior tourists. Whereas Dr. Ravi is worried about the supposedly fragile physical condition of the future clients of Dunroamin Retirement Hotel, of the long distance that would separate them from their family and friends, Sonny insists on the fact that older people are also sophisticated travellers nowadays, as he tells Ravi: "We're all global travellers now, old boy, cheap packages to God knows where, Maldives, Seychelles, our own beauteous state of Kerala, cheaper than Connex bloody South-East to Worthing and probably faster too [...] Who wants to be stuck there in some nasty little room smelling of cabbage?" (19). And when Pauline, Dr. Ravi's wife, insists on the fact that "Old people like the familiar", Ravi answers "What's familiar about the world they live in now? Britain's a foreign country to most of them these days, it's frightening, it's confusing—" (20). Thus, on the one hand, Dunroamin Retirement Hotel is a new opportunity for the future residents but, on the other hand, it reflects the fact that British society, Western society as an extension, is still not ready to assume the fact that it is an ageing society and, as a consequence, old age and ageing have to be included within the day to day life as well as future planning of such a society. As a good businessman who can envisage the flaws of society in order to set up successful businesses, Sonny realises that he can offer a better life to British senior citizens. As he explains Pauline and Ravi, "'Big bucks all round, and a benefit to humanity. Sounds good so far, eh?" (17).

The character of Sonny and the reasons behind the setting up of the hotel are quite different in the film version. Sonny is presented as a young man who has inherited a run-down hotel from his father and who has this implausible idea of turning it into a first-class hotel in order to honour his father's memory. Thus, the business-like and clever Sonny of the novel is presented in a romanticised way since the young Sonny of the film is presented as a dreamy and inexperienced character. This also contributes to present a more idealistic relationship between the older characters and Sonny as manager of the hotel. In fact, some of the older characters in the film, such as Muriel and Madge, take a paternalistic role towards Sonny when they decide to help him to run the hotel and to make his mum accept the relationship he has with a young Indian woman who is not the wife his family had set up for him. In this sense, the novel presents a more ironic, sometimes even acid, image of the fact that the protagonists had to move to India in front of the poor perspectives of staying in their native country. To give an example, at the beginning of the novel, Muriel Donnelly, one of the older protagonists, becomes one of the protagonists of England's tabloids for one day when she has to spend two days on a trolley after having been mugged and injured: "[p]hotos showed her lolling grey head and black eye. Plucky pensioner, she had survived the Blitz for this? Her image was beamed around the country" (3). Even though Muriel did not get immediate attention at the hospital because she would not let any coloured doctor touch her, the comparison between old age and the Blitz in this sentence enhances the bitter sweet meaning of the fact that, despite having survived a World War, British and Western society is not ready to face an exponentially ageing population. Actually, Sonny defines "[t]he pensions time bomb!" as "a disaster of epic proportions" when he is trying to convince Ravi to become his business partner. He is convinced that England is neither ready nor willing to face the consequences of an ageing population and he is ready to take advantage of it for his business interests.

INDIA: A NEW LEASE OF LIFE

Sonny envisages and advertises Dunroamin Retirement Hotel as a piece of Britain but with two important positive differences: a sunnier weather and a relaxed and carefree atmosphere where British citizens will forget about the pressures of old age, both physical and economic. The retirement home is actually presented as an attractive holidays destination directed to senior citizens, despite the fact that the period the British citizens may spend may be an indefinite period of time:

> The Dunroamin Retirement Hotel combines the tranquillity of yesteryear with exciting shopping and sightseeing opportunities. Enjoy the ambiance of a bygone age with the advantages of modern living: all rooms, both de-luxe and standard, are equipped with direct-dial telephones and Star TV. First-class cuisine includes both English and South Indian specialities. Come and pamper yourself! You deserve it. (23)

Moving to India has positive effects for the protagonists of the novel and film. Once in India, the older characters who decide to spend their retirement years there start changing their English standards in terms of appropriateness and acceptability. They realise that everything depends on the perspective one looks at things and, so does old age and what old age is supposed to imply. In fact, the bearer in the hotel, a man called Jimmy who seemed to be on permanent duty, was older than most of the guests. While Evelyn observes him moving around the hall, she realises that "[h]is advanced age made Evelyn feel like a spring chicken. In England, no doubt, he would long since have been put out to grass. In India, however, people seemed to carry on until they dropped" (105). After the death of her husband, Evelyn realised she was old and that there was not much left for her to do. While talking to a younger beautician, her only friend after her husband's death, about the options she could contemplate as a widower, Evelyn reflects "[t]his life, it's as if I'm dead already" (45). Evelyn had been a wife and a mum for a long time and, thus, she only conceived herself within these two roles. In India, she realises that she can still be useful to society outside those roles when she accepts to help a group of young people who work at a call centre by telling them about the 'real' England. Moreover, feelings she had thought forgotten and buried, and not really appropriate after youth, reappear again when she starts feeling a close connection to Douglas Ainslie.

Muriel, by her part, had always been a proper Cockney lady, practical and upright, who did not trust "darkies" (58). However, once in India she starts a close relationship with the wife of one of the owners of the hotel, Razia, who introduces her into the spiritual side of India which she takes as if it had always been part of herself. As Evelyn observes,

The irony was that despite her prejudices Muriel had sopped up more Indian ways than any of them. [...] Muriel seemed to have absorbed subcontinental beliefs straight into her bloodstream; it seemed to answer something in her nature. She regularly read her horoscope with Mrs Cowasjee [...]; she had had her fortune told by the man with the parrot in the bazaar opposite. The scent of joss-sticks drifted from her room and Stella swore that she had heard her chanting some incantation (138).

After the string of implausible events that bring Muriel to India, she starts believing in the fact that everything is connected to everything else and, thus, she also starts believing in karma. For the first time in her life, she realises that anything one does may have consequences beyond rational explanation. The character of Muriel Donelly is a clear opposition to the stereotype that a person in old age is unable to change and open their minds. As Hepworth and Wernick argue in their introduction to *Images of Ageing. Cultural Representations of Later Life*, "images of ageing represent bodies which become increasingly fixed and inflexible as they move towards the end of the life course" (11). In the case of Muriel, a series of events together with the personal circumstances in which she finds herself—being alone and having been mugged in the middle of the day, her son being chased by the police, her house being burglared and cat killed, and having no close family and friends—make Muriel look at the world from a different perspective. Indeed, the fact of moving to India, of having to adapt to a new environment and new people also contributes to this change. However, Muriel's questioning of her identity and status as an old British citizen starts when she realises that her own cultural image of a proper working-class retired British lady crumbles when no one in her country can offer her solace or security for her remaining years. In *The Best Exotic Marigold Hotel*, Muriel is also depicted as an upright British lady who decides to move to India, temporarily, in order to get an affordable hip replacement. The reasons behind her moving to the hotel are also related to a shattering welfare state which cannot account for an ageing population. In the film, it is even more graphically shown how she goes from being a British woman with limiting conceptions on race and nationality to picture and set herself in a different role. The Muriel Donnely of *The Best Exotic Marigold Hotel* is very good with numbers and she actually starts helping the dreamy Sonny of the film in setting up a successful business. By the end of the film, she decides to stay in India and become the assistant manager of the Hotel. Muriel not only overcomes her own prejudices and limiting conceptions on race, gender and age but she also adopts a useful and active role within her adoptive community. Following Margaret Gullette's arguments in *Aged by Culture*, ageing and old age have been conceived, told and repeated as narratives of decline in Western society. As Gullette explains, "the narrative of decline involved unconscious habits of thought and affected every subidentity, ways of seeing bodies and holding one's own, explanations of history [...] it distorted visual culture" (28). In this respect, the character of Muriel Donelly in both Moggach's *These Foolish Things* and its film version challenges the declining narrative of a British woman in her seventies who lives alone in a big city. Ironically enough, moving away from her native background allows Muriel to change her personal declining narrative for a narrative in which she overcomes her own restricting cultural believes and pictures herself in a productive and creative role.

In India, the characters Norman and Madge do not have to hide their sexual instincts; on the contrary, they can express themselves openly without being judged or misunderstood. In fact, in *These Foolish Things*, Sonny takes Madge to an elegant party so that she can be introduced to a rich and handsome Indian man and, over time, she actually finds a boyfriend. By his part, Sonny helps Norman to have one last night of wild sex, although the old protagonist actually dies of a heart attack during the event. One of the limiting stereotypes related to old age is the fact that desire and sexuality have somehow dried and, thus, it is not appropriate to feel them after a certain age. In an article entitled "'That's very Rude, I Shouldn't be Telling you That': Older Women Talking about Sex", Rebecca L. Jones proves that the "dominant cultural storyline" (125) that asserts that old people have lost interest in sex by interviewing twenty-three respondents, thirteen of which claimed to have a sexual active life after the age of sixty. In this sense, the characters of Norman and Madge belief that moving to India will allow them to move away from restrictive beliefs related to old age and sex. As Norman reflects to himself once set in Dunroamin Retirement Hotel, "[h]is carnal knowledge of Indian women was limited—to be frank, non-existent—but he knew they were tutored in sexual wiles from an early age and the prostate doctor's words had inflamed him. Surely here, in India, he could arouse his flagging libido?" (94).

Actually, the sexual instincts of all the female characters who move to Dunroamin Retirement Hotel are stirred by the appearance of Dr Rama. The first time he visits the hotel, Dr. Rama is described as a "even more dazzling, however, in real life; more dazzling, even, than Omar Sharif in his prime. [...] There was a hush, then a fluttering sound, like hens settling down" (124). Later that night, "the residents slumbered, dreaming of Dr. Rama who lifted their nighties with his caring brown hands" (128). Any time Dr. Rama appeared in the hotel, the bodily nuances caused by the advanced age of the female residents at Dunroamin Retirement Hotel disappeared for a while and were substituted by feelings of desire and sexual admiration. In this respect, Moggach seems to question one of the most recurrent roles attached to ageing and old age, that is, illness and infirmity[2]. Without negating the biological ageing of the body which is present through the inner monologues and conversations with other residents, Dr. Rama has the effect of making the female residents in the hotel forget those nuances for a while and, the boldest female residents, actually use them as an excuse to set up a visit with Dr. Rama. Even though the scenes in which Dr. Rama appears have a humorous halo, through them, the novel undermines the roles of illness and infirmity attached to an old population. Moreover, this limiting conception of old age is questioned again in relation to Norman's death. Norman dies because he had overmedicated himself with Viagra before meeting the prostitute with whom Sonny had set up a date. This, together with the excitement of having a sexual en-

---

2 | In *Learning to Be Old. Gender, Culture and Aging*, Margaret Cruickshank theorises on the "sick role" (35) of the old. According to Cruickshank, industrial countries induce old people, also the healthy ones, to adopt the sick role since the old are "conditioned to believe that aging is a disease requiring heavy consumption of medical services" (36). In *Old Age, Constructions and Deconstructions*, Haim Hazan also refers to illness as a role that the aged are expected to follow.

counter and the surprise of realising that his date was a man instead of a woman, causes the stop of Norman's heart. As Madge explains, "it was called *le petit mort*" (231).

Douglas Ainslie is another of the characters who starts questioning his life path, his expected role as a married retired man, which does not match his real expectations and, thus, he ends up questioning and changing his own cultural standards once in India. Despite the fact that he and his wife Jean had travelled in their previous retirement years, it is the fact of moving to India which makes him realise he wanted to express himself openly and follow his own desires without being constantly aware of projecting a specific social image. As he himself reflects, "[s]omething in this country answered a certain lassitude in his soul. It was the enervating weight of the place, the mass of its humanity who couldn't do anything about anything either" (171). Tired of pretending to be the perfect British family and to be living a successful old age, as if their moving to India had been the result of their adventurous personality and fashionable way of life, instead of the result of feeling lonely and without enough economic resources, he decides to leave Jean and start a relationship with Evelyn. Being in India, makes Douglas realise that after having dedicated a long time to try to make Jean happy, silencing his own interests, "[h]e didn't mind how she felt, the woman with whom he had shared his life for forty-eight years. *I don't mind. I don't care. In fact, I don't even like her*" (171). In his old age and far from his native country, Douglas uncovers the path he actually wants to follow leaving to a side social and community constraints.

Conclusion

In both Deborah Moggach's novel and its film version, in India and within the context of the hotel, the older British characters can relax and forget about the way they are supposed to be and behave due to their age, gender and social class. Thus, their conception of old age and ageing as well as the relationships they establish with their peers and their family members is modified. For the first time in many years, they can focus on enjoying new experiences and coming to terms with their real expectations and hopes as people who are travelling along a continuous life course—not just as people in old age, a static stage. In India, getting involved in the reality of the country and the different ways in which life and death are perceived, the old protagonists become aware that life is a gift which cannot be spoilt in narrowing constraints and endless complaints. As Madge explains by the end of the novel,

'It's been go-go-go these past few weeks,' Madge whispered to her new boyfriend, whose name was Mr Desikachar.' Dorothy told the Ainslies their son was gay, the manager kicked out his wife, the cook's gone, the doctor's gone, an old soak called Norman died in a brothel but his daughter doesn't know, she thinks he was bying her a Christmas present. And that's just for starters.'
'I thought this was a Retirement Home,' said Mr Desikachar.
'Life begins at seventy.' Madge smiled, dazzling him with her expensive dentistry. 'Seventy's the new forty, didn't you know? (261)

At another level, the novel poses the question of why this looking at old age from a wider perspective and at the life course as a continuum cannot be achieved in their native countries. Moving to India makes both protagonists and readers and viewers question pre-established stereotypes attached to old age; namely, the fact of being unable to change and develop new interests and holding on to the "sick role" instead, and being unable to feel neither desire nor sexual interest. In both Moggach's novel and its film version, the main characters undermine these stereotypes by changing their personal cultural images in terms of the ageing experience but also in terms of nationality. Moreover, while discovering the city as well as coming to terms with their new situation, they leave their minor illnesses to a side, using them only to come close to attractive Dr. Rama. On the other hand, they actually adopt new active roles within the community in which they come to be part. By moving to India, Muriel, Evelyn, Douglas and Madge give a new direction to their life narratives and turn them into development narratives, rather than decline ones.

Going back to the theoretical background related to senior tourism presented in the first section of this article, *These Foolish Things* and its film version can be read as presenting an alternative view of senior tourism closer to the integrating model presented by Hunter-Jones and Blackburn in which senior tourism moves beyond the reproduction of a sunnier Britain and offers an enriching experience in which older citizens are asked to interact actively and, thus, become the protagonists of building the remaining episodes of their life narratives. Through an ironic and humorous tone in which serious and critical concerns are ingrained in front of the exponential ageing of Western population, Deborah Moggach offers a plausible but not completely satisfactory answer to such concerns. Ultimately, cultural constraining believes attached to the experience of ageing and old age are brought to the surface and are questioned and undermined when the same characters decide to embrace the choices that being away from their native country seems to offer them.

WORKS CITED

Blaikie, Andrew. *Ageing and Popular Culture*. Cambridge University Press, 1999. Print.

Chaney, David. "Creating Memories. Some Images of Aging in Mass Tourism". Ed. Mike Featherstone and Andrew Wernick. *Images of Aging. Cultural Representations of Later Life*. London: Routledge, 1995. 213-30 Print.

Elias, Norbert. *The Loneliness of the Dying*. New York: Basil Blackwell, 1985. Print.

Featherstone, Mike and Andrew Wernick, eds. *Images of Ageing. Cultural Representations of Later Life*. London: Routledge, 1995. Print.

Featherstone, Mike and Mike Hepworth. "Images of Ageing." *Ageing in Society. An Introduction to Social Gerontology.* Ed John Bond. Sage Publications: London, 1990. 304-32. Print.

—. "Images of Positive Aging: A Case Study of *Retirement Choice Magazine.*" *Images of Aging. Cultural Representations of Later Life.* Eds. Mike Featherstone and Andrew Wernick. London: Routledge, 1995. 27-46. Print.

Gullette, Margaret Moganroth. *Aged by Culture.* The University of Chicago Press, 2004. Print.

Hazan, Haim. *Old Age, Constructions and Deconstructions.* Cambridge: Cambridge UP, 1994. Print.

Hunter-Jones, Philippa and Adele Blackburn. "Understanding the relationship between holiday taking and self-assessed health: an exploratory study of senior tourism". *International Journal of Consumer Studies.* 31 (2007): 509-16.

Jones, Rebecca L. "That's very Rude, I Shouldn't be Telling you That:" Older Women Talking about Sex. *Narrative Inquiry.* 12.1 (2002): 121-43.

Lohmann, Martin and Johanna Danielsson. "Predicting travel patterns of senior citizens: How the past may provide a key to the future." *Journal of Vacation Marketing.* 7.4 (2001): 357-66.

Moggach, Deborah. *These Foolish Things.* London, Chatto & Windus, 2004. Print.

Patterson, I. and S. Pegg. "Ageing Travellers: Seeking an Experience—Not Just a Destination." *Accessible Tourism. Concepts and Issues.* Ed. Dimitrios Buhalis and Simon Darcy. Bristol: Chanel View Publications, 2011. 174-90. Print.

The Best Exotic Marigold Hotel. Dir. John Madden. Writ. Ol Parker and Deborah Moggach. 2011. DVD.

Walker, Tim. "Deborah Moggah: Elderly should take a passage to India". *The Telegraph.* 18 April 2011. Web. 16 December 2014.

The Older You Are, the More Sustainable You Get

A Sociological Snapshot of Cultural Tourism at an Eastern Adriatic "Living Heritage Site"

Mirko Petrić, Ivan Puzek, Inga Tomić-Koludrović

Recent years have seen a continual increase in importance of the two categories at the heart of the discussion in the essay that follows: "aging tourists" and "living heritage site". Tourism is nowadays universally referred to as the world's largest commercial service sector industry. In this context, the segments of a generally aging population (especially baby boomers in rich Western countries) and attractions covered by the umbrella term "cultural tourism" are frequently seen as potential engines of its further growth.

In the area of heritage protection, the notion of "living heritage site" has become increasingly prominent in the 21st century, although UNESCO's World Heritage Convention, which came into effect in 1972, already made reference to the "life of a community" at a given heritage site. In the new socio-cultural and economic context, there happened a shift from a previous focus on identification of the monuments of world importance to the current focus on site management and conservation in the context of development. With such a change in mind, it is only logical that sustainability issues have also come to the forefront, especially since tourism—the main industry linked to heritage sites—is also a primary cause of their environmental and socio-cultural degradation.

The text that follows is a brief case study of how the aging tourists can help sustain the essential qualities of a living heritage site. It is based on the comparison of primary data obtained by the surveys of tourists visiting the historical core of the UNESCO-protected Eastern Adriatic coast city of Split, carried out in the years 2005 and 2013. Different types of tourists, their motivations and cultural consumption are discussed against the backdrop of what UNESCO refers to as "outstanding universal value" of the discussed site. References are also made to the data and insights gained by the comprehensive research of various other aspects of the site, carried out in 2013 for the purpose of completion of the draft management plan for the "historical complex of Split with the Palace of Diocletian" (Petrić et al, 2016).

In the process, it is hoped that a more profound understanding will be gained of an important aspect (socio-cultural sustainability) of the complex relationship between a world heritage site and the visiting tourists. Furthermore, given the prominence in the analysis of the aging tourists, it is hoped that this essay will also be a contribution to a better understanding of the importance of the role of this segment of the tourist population at selected locations, in terms of their specific contribution to the sustainability of the local culture and to the quality of life of a community in general.

To that end, we first describe the heritage qualities of the city of Split, present a brief outline of the history of tourism on the Eastern Adriatic coast, and discuss the problems connected with the recent explosion of interest in urban tourism. Following that, we outline the data obtained by the cited 2005 and 2013 surveys of the tourists visiting the historic core of Split and discuss the differences in their findings. Finally, based on this discussion, we explain why we think that aging tourists can be a highly desirable and "sustainable" group of visitors for compact city cores of heritage sites.

Given the case study approach to the subject matter, it goes without saying that the possibilities of generalization are severely limited. However, it is hoped that the interpretation of the presented data can be useful in roughly comparable contexts and illustrate the aspects of sustainability not frequently encountered in the discussions of senior tourism. The purpose of this essay is to serve as a contribution to what Levine refers to as "sociological snapshots", i.e. to provide a relational contextual explanation grounded in one concrete example. This particular "snapshot" will doubtlessly be of interest to the citizens and policy makers in the heritage cities exposed to intensive tourist exploitation, but we hope it can also deliver useful insights to aging studies scholars and to social scientists in general.

Heritage qualities of and contemporary challenges in the historical core of Split

"Historical Complex of Split with the Palace of Diocletian" was inscribed on UNESCO's World Heritage List in 1979, following a nomination that made due mention of its architectural and urban qualities, but also emphasized the continued existence of the site as a human settlement from the late Antiquity to the present day.

In the description currently featured on World Heritage List web pages dedicated to the site, it is mentioned that the ruins of the palace erected by the Roman Emperor Diocletian between the late 3rd and the early 4th centuries A.D. can be found throughout the heritage core of the present day city of Split. The rest of the UNESCO-protected area of the "historical complex of Split" comprises the cathedral built in the Middle Ages, 12th and 13th century Romanesque churches, medieval fortifications, 15th-century Gothic palaces and other palaces in Renaissance and Baroque style.

However, in spite of the individual architectural and artistic qualities of all these buildings (as well as its considerable influence on subsequent developments in urbanism and architecture ranging from those in the Dalmatian region and other places in the Mediterranean to the Neoclassical period of British architecture) what is referred to by UNESCO as "outstanding universal value" of the site derives primarily from its already mentioned continued existence as an urban area ever since it was transformed from the Roman imperial palace into a living medieval city in the Early Middle Ages. In addition to being the best preserved complex of its type, the Palace of Diocletian is the only late imperial palace that has remained in use as a habitation to the present day.[1]

In many ways, the 1979 UNESCO World Heritage list nomination for the so-labeled "Historical Complex of Split with the Palace of Diocletian" can be seen as prefiguring the current "people-centered approaches to the conservation of cultural heritage", effectively summarized by Court and Wijesuriya, and especially the notion of "living heritage", which Wijesuriya (1) describes as being marked primarily by the concept of "continuity", and "in particular the continuity of a heritage site's original function".

In contrast with the dominant terminology of the past regarding heritage, continues the same author, which centered on the debates on living vs. dead monuments, and the predilection of the formative conservation discourse for the latter, the current conservation discourse is focused on the notion of "living heritage", linked to "communities" and the "continuity" of tradition and practices. Wijesuriya also highlights the fact that, in this new optics, the so-called "core community", living on the heritage site, is also considered responsible for the continuous care of its heritage aspects and for the management of change, which is now also considered to be a part of the heritage conservation efforts.

It is exactly in this aspect that the current situation of the "Historical Complex of Split with the Palace of Diocletian" is beginning to deteriorate both in relation to a pronounced component of its original "outstanding universal value" (that effectively represented a prefiguration of the notion of the "living heritage site") and with respect to the requirements of contemporary site management. Namely, as

---

1 | The identification of the "outstanding universal value" of the "historical complex of Split with the Palace of Diocletian" summarized in this paragraph follows the draft declaration recently sent to UNESCO for verification by the Ministry of Culture of the Republic of Croatia and published in the Draft Management Plan (Petrić et al, 12-13).

is noted in the 2016 Draft Management Plan for the Historical Core of Split and the Substructures of the Palace of Diocletian (275-307), the UNESCO-protected area has lost 28% of its permanent residents between the population censuses carried out in 2001 and 2011, and the depopulation of the area has continued in the years following the 2011 census at an ever faster rate. In some micro-zones of the area, the depopulation of younger people (aged 15-29) stood at as much as 48% in 2011 (299).

The reasons behind these developments are real estate speculation and intensifying mass tourism, making permanent living in the area close to unbearable. The depopulation trends are changing the daily routines of those living in situ, and are consequently depriving the site of the "continuity of traditions and practices" valued in the contemporary conservation discourse, while mass tourism wears out the physical infrastructure and endangers what has earlier been referred to as "dead monuments".

Findings of recent empirical research of tourists visiting the historical core of Split suggest that aging tourists can be seen as the segment of the tourist population that actually contributes to the maintenance of some of the highly valued characteristics of this heritage site, or—in the contemporary policy discourse—to its "sustainability". However, to be able to explain why such a suggestion can be made, we first have to present a brief outline of the historical and current tourist trends on the Eastern Adriatic coast and in the city of Split itself, as well as to thematize the relationship between cultural tourism and sustainability.

FROM GRAND TOUR TO PARTY AND CRUISE TOURISM: THE CITY AS A STAGE SET?

The history of tourism in the city of Split in many ways differs significantly from that of other well-known destinations in the Eastern Adriatic. The history of modern tourism in these parts can be said to have begun in the mid-1850s on the stretch of the coastline in the

Northern Adriatic known as the Riviera of Opatija (ital. Abbazia), which attracted visitors from the Habsburg Empire because of the alleged curative properties of its fresh sea air and flourished as a climatic resort for the elites at the turn of the century. In the inter-war period (1918-1939), tourism as a form of economic activity spread southward and catered to the interests of tourists coming predominantly from the industrially developed countries of Central Europe. Among the visitors, however, were also interested individual travelers from English-speaking countries, frequently writers and intellectuals, or members of the propertied classes.

Following the destructions of World War II and the initial period of the newly established Yugoslavia's socialist regime, in which the country was largely closed to foreign influence, there followed a cultural and economic opening to the West, which resulted in the fast development in the 1960s and 1970s of a mass tourism of the "sun and sea" type along the entire Eastern Adriatic coast. In this period, the most frequent foreign visitors to the region were either of working class background or were recognizable as the members of what the sociologist Helmut Schelsky described in the years of the German postwar economic miracle as "leveled middle-class society". In the context of senior tourism, it is worth noting that in the 1970s the British agency Saga, organizing off-peak holidays exclusively for retired people, expanded its operations to the destinations in what was then socialist Yugoslavia.

Finally, in the most recent period, following the wars of Yugoslav succession in the first half of the 1990s, which brought about a temporary cessation of tourist activities, a new profile of East Adriatic tourism began to emerge in the late 1990s and early 2000s, and was then fully developed by the 2010s. In addition to family tourism, dominant in the area in the second half of the 20th century, in this period there appeared cruise tourism as a new form of mass tourism, but also various forms of niche tourism, as well as unprecedented levels of luxury on selected destinations. As regards the profiles of visitors, in this period there ensued their significant diversification, in accordance with the process of individualization in what Ulrich

Beck (1986) described as "second modernity" trends, taking place in economically and technologically advanced countries. In relation to the previous period, in which family tourism of working class and "leveled middle-class" profiles of visitors from European—and most frequently Central European—countries dominated in the area, it is now also visited by large numbers of individualized tourists of different ages and levels of income from all around the world.

To a great extent, these trends in different periods were reflected in the development of tourism in the city of Split. However, due to the early recognition of the outstanding value of its cultural heritage, the historical trajectory of tourism in Split has followed a path somewhat at odds with those found elsewhere on the Eastern Adriatic coast. In the periods preceding the post-World War 2 expansion of mass tourism, Split differed from other cities on the coast in that it attracted the Grand Tour type of visitors: among them were visual artists who made the ruins of the Palace of Diocletian an inspiration for the development of architecture elsewhere. Most famously, the five-week visit of the Scottish architect Robert Adam and the French architectural draftsman Charles-Louis Clérisseau in 1757, and the ensuing book on the *Ruins of the Palace of the Emperor Diocletian at Spalatro in Dalmatia* (1764) exerted a decisive influence on the development of British Neoclassical architecture. Visits of intellectuals and political figures, whose travel writings have recently attracted increasing academic and public attention, following their analyses by Pederin, Wild Bićanić, Levačić and others, continued all the way to the end of the interwar period.

While architectural experts continued to visit Split throughout the post-World War 2 period, the profile of run-of-the-mill cultural tourists in this period did not resemble that of the distinguished visitors from more remote past. Although the Grand Tour type of visitors are sometimes seen as a sort of cultural tourists *avant la lettre*, the cultural tourists in the golden age of mass tourism in Yugoslavia certainly lacked their intellectual and artistic aspirations. Instead, tourists who visited Split in the 1960s and 1970s with cultural and heritage motivations can be described as wanting more an illustration of knowledge acquired in the secondary or initial post-secondary period of their education, in a social context in which such a confirmation of "general knowledge" and "general culture" still mattered as a form of distinction. In practice, this meant that so-called "stationary tourists", spending their "sun and sea" type of holidays in hotels on nearby islands or coastal riviera, most frequently visited the heritage core of Split in the form of organized day trips or while waiting for their transfers to further destinations.

Following a complete cessation of tourist activities in the most intense period of wars of Yugoslav succession,[2] visits to Split in the late 1990s and in the first half of the 2000s were largely reduced to cursory sightseeing at a stopover location. In this period, the perception of Split as predominantly a transfer point for further destinations was strengthened almost to the point of neglect not only of its heritage riches but also of its urban qualities and atmosphere.

However, by the mid-2000s, such a state of things began to change as new types of visitors appeared in the historical core of Split. Tomić-Koludrović and Petrić (2007), who carried out a comprehensive survey researching the motivation of visitors in 2005,[3] concluded that among them were many of those who were best described as "new cultural tourists", not interested primarily in "dead monuments" but in experiencing the authenticity of the city atmosphere. These tourists, who were on the average younger than the rest of the visitors to Eastern Adriatic destinations, were also better educated, frequently traveled on their own, and already at that time used Internet-based information channels and advice of friends as the

---

2 | According to Ashbrook (2011), what is described by the term "Wars of Yugoslav Succession" relates to four major conflicts that took place in Slovenia, Croatia, Bosnia-Herzegovina, and Serbia-Kosovo, and lasted from 1990 to 1999. What is referred to in this chapter as "the most intense period of wars of Yugoslav succession" relates to the conflicts in Croatia and Bosnia-Herzegovina in the first half of the 1990s.

3 | The survey was funded by the British Council, as part of its UK-South East Europe Forum.

primary source of learning about the city. Also, the survey results indicated that these visitors preferred to rent rooms and apartments from the locals to hotel accommodation, not only because that was more affordable but also because that way they hoped to learn more about the local way of life.

By means of cluster analysis of the visitors to the heritage core of the city of Split, three types were identified, differing principally in the motives of their visit and in the activities they engaged in during their stay on location. The first type comprised visitors interested in cultural events and aiming to learn more about themselves by means of interaction with the new surroundings. The second type was more interested in the life of cultural monuments on their actual location, as well as in the local way of life in general. The third type was made up of those who wanted primarily to "recharge batteries" by means of recreation on nearby islands and mountains. The visitors who belonged to this latter type also visited cultural monuments, when they realized that they were there and that they were world famous, but this was not the primary motivation of their visit. It should also be remarked that the ambition to "recharge batteries" in the period at hand did not correspond to the entertainment profile of the so-called "party tourists", but were more inward-directed and individualized.

The profile of visitors, even in the case of the recreation-oriented type, was doubtlessly in tune with the tendency towards individualization and striving for authenticity and meaning in the search for the self. Atter a certain delay, due to the 1990s wars in the region, the city of Split obviously experienced a high increase in the number of visitors who were part of the trends succinctly summarized by Lord (1999) at the end of that decade. According to the data presented in her quoted speech (4), illustrating what she described as a "shift from escapism to enrichment", it is evident that in comparison with the 1980s, in the subsequent decade the percentages of tourists seeking to "experience a completely different culture", "go off the beaten track", "visit a place they have never been to before", "gain new perspective on life", "understand culture", or simply visit "cultural, historical or archaeological treasures", increased from 33% to more than 50%.

It is also worth mentioning that Lord attributed the changing trends to rising education levels, increasing economic role of women, and a generally aging population, arguing with regard to the latter that people in the age range between 45 and 65 are known to be "typically in their peak learning years and have the highest discretionary income and time to spend on culture related activities and travel" (5). The fact that in the historical core of Split, in the first half of the 2000s, the visitors with described priorities were on the whole younger, could be attributed to the still lingering uneasiness of the older age groups about visiting a previously war-affected area, as well as their assumption that the standards of accommodation would be lower than their normal expectations. However, all the other elements found by Lord to be characteristic of the "emerging trends impacting cultural tourism" were found in Split in the mid-2000s: "increase in get-away trips", "impact of 'Gen-X tourists'" (i.e. of those born between 1965 and 1977), "emphasis on meaning", "increasing expectations", "desire for sustainability", an interest in "events", and "impact of the Internet" (7).

The yearning for authenticity and enrichment, coupled with the wish to understand local cultures and contribute to their sustainability, was obviously in harmony with the idea of the "living heritage site" and "people-centered approaches to the conservation of cultural heritage". Unfortunately, the change of trends following the 2008 global financial crisis has also brought with it changes in the types of visitors to the heritage core of Split, resulting in a significant change in their motivations and priorities. This change can generally be described as going in the direction of increasingly equating the experiential component of traveling with consumerism.

In other words, the trends noted in the Split area following the global financial crisis can be seen as a sign of a renewed massification of the tourist experience for a part of the visitors. Such trends are arguably attributable to an abrupt leap in the number of culturally less-aspiring visitors from cruise ships, as well as to the increased presence in the city core of predominantly younger "party tourists", seeking entertainment events and frequently coming with a specific intention to take part in what is known as "pub crawl tours".

As regards the number of day visitors from cruise ships, there was a fifteen-fold increase in their number in the period between 2002 and 2012, and according to data presented in Petrić et al (495-496), this increase was particularly strongly felt between 2005 (when there were 50 thousand cruise ship visitors) and 2012 (when there were 320 thousand visits). On the other hand, as regards an even further increase in the number of younger tourists, it can be said to be in line with global trends.[4] What has crystalized as the specificity

---

4 | According to the 2013 World Youth Student and Educational Travel Confederation study ("New Horizons III", WYSE), in 2012 youth travelers represented no less than 20 per cent of international tourism. The report put an emphasis on the fact that the spending of this segment of the tourist population increased by 40% since 2007. Furthermore, it was stressed in the report that the rise in spending of youth travelers outstripped by far that of other segments of international tourists, making them an important economic force. The WYSE report also established that there existed an increasing complexity and segmentation of youth and student travel market, with many young people increasingly traveling to gain cultural competences improving their education and work prospects. On the other hand, in the context of this publication, one should not fail to mention that, according to a recent Eurostat news release, "tourists aged 65 or over [...] living in the European Union (EU) accounted for 20% of the tourism activity (in terms of number of nights spent by EU residents)" (1). This amounts to exactly the same share of tourism activity of EU residents as the one reported by WYSE for the participation of young travelers in international tourism. What is more, "older tourists", as they are referred to by Eurostat make the largest age category in the quoted report, since the share of younger travelers was divided into two groups (tourists aged 15-24 made 14 per cent, and those aged 25-34 15 per cent of the sample). By any measure, it is beyond doubt that these two categories ("young travelers" and "older tourists") are growing fastest on the European market.

of Split in the 2010s is the overwhelming dominance of the mentioned party-oriented tourists (locally erroneously known under the umbrella term "backpackers"[5]) in the peak summer months.

---

5 | One should note here that the term "backpackers" is by no means used to denote primarily (or even exclusively) "party tourists", although the latter group seems to be the most visible one and to receive most media attention in the case of young visitors in the city core of Split. Rather, the term "backpacker" is used to generally denote younger travelers displaying "a common commitment to a non-institutionalised form of travel", emphasized as "central to their self-identification" by qualitative researchers such as Adkins and Grant (189). Motivations of a large number of these travelers, relying on low cost means of transportation and inexpensive (hostel) lodging, are actually cultural and educational. A usually longer duration of their trips, as well as the proclaimed "search for authenticity", actually make their stays at heritage sites comparable to a mass version of the Grand Tour experience. Likewise, one should also not forget the fraction of the "backpacker" segment forming in the 2000s that goes by the name "flashpackers": this term refers to those traveling with a backpacker ethos but usually somewhat older, on a higher budget, and bringing along "flashier" laptops and other gadgets. Finally, average age of backpackers has been continually increasing, and it is now common not only for people in their thirties and forties, but also for some retirees to engage in this type of traveling. Our observations show that all these types of "backpackers" visit the heritage core of Split, but have in recent years been overshadowed in high season by "party types", making the term "backpackers" locally synonymous with "young", "little spending", "loud" and generally obnoxious tourists, especially destructive of the location's distinctive atmosphere (genius loci). In actuality, our observations indicate that, although many among them carry backpacks and wear comparable clothes, what goes locally as "backpackers" in Split could be more precisely described as a sort of extended city break tourists with budgets somewhat below average in that category, who are frequently party-motivated and engage in short (i.e. lasting only a couple of days) "island hopping" as a sort of "extended" or "after" party experience. What makes these tourists different from the usual city break

New heights for these kinds of visits were reached following the choice of Split as the European location of the global multi-venue outdoor electronic music festival Ultra in 2013. Locally, in the historical city core, the flurry of backpacking and party visitors alike has brought the already developing trends of "hostelization" and "apartmanization" to a new level. What these neologisms refer to is the turning of the previously inhabited parts of the city into gentrified enclaves offering what used to be private apartments for short-term rent to tourists, frequently through Internet rental services or online marketplace sites. Such developments, driving out the local residents from what previously were their homes, have accelerated the already existing depopulation trends, turning what used to be a living part of the city into a stage set for tourist sightseeing or entertainment. Coupled with an increase in the spectacularization of heritage, most prominently through costumed performances for the new mass tourists, such "uses of the city" are obviously at odds with UNESCO's and ICCROM's idea of "living heritage site", once prefigured exactly by the "life of the community" in the historical city core of Split and its continual dialogue with the contemporaneity.

---

visitors is that their trips take place in the summer months, while city break visits usually take place all year round. In other words, although partly similar in visual outlook, "party types" in the city core of Split have aspirations completely, or at least largely, different from those typical of the 1990s and pre-2008 "backpackers". The crucial difference between the two seems to be that "party types" are less or differently "self-oriented". Using Riesman's classical distinction between "inner-directed" and "other-directed" people, their "social character" could be described as more conforming to the latter, i.e. as guided more by external pressures than by their own set of values. The "party types" currently visible in the city core of Split actually seem to be the children of the post-2008 crisis period, and their activities seem to be a lower-class, youthful imitation of what they imagine to be "having fun while away" of those more affluent (and older) than themselves. Needless to say, these initial observations of ours need to be verified by further empirical research.

The question is: what is to be done, if the current status and presently largely compromised heritage qualities of the UNESCO-protected area are to be preserved or, rather, reinstated? Apart from the need for stronger local regulation of the processes in the city core, resulting in the increase of the characteristic former local uses of this area, one would obviously need to try to regulate tourist flows and to attract more "sustainable" types of visitors. With this in mind, the question again is: who would these more "sustainable" and "responsible" tourists be, and are they already present to some degree among the current visitors?

THE OLDER YOU GET, THE MORE SUSTAINABLE YOU ARE?

Attempting to provide answers to these questions, we now turn to the results of a comprehensive survey of tourists who visited the historical core of Split in 2013, carried out in two waves (in high season and off-peak), as well as to the survey of museum visitors carried out during a peak period of the same year.[6] The cluster analysis of the first mentioned survey helped us identify the types of tourists visiting the historical core of Split in 2013, while the survey of museum visitors and street-level observations carried out in the same period, helped us fine-tune a part of our interpretations.

Following the analysis of empirical data, a more complex picture emerges, although—in terms of sheer numbers—the impressions of local residents and media about the dominance of party and cruise ship tourists in the city core are certainly not wrong. Likewise, the impression that Split is mostly visited by younger tourists is supported by empirical data: our 2013 survey has shown that almost a quarter (24%) of the surveyed visitors to the historical core of Split were aged 16 to 24, while a further 33% of the visitors were aged 26 to 35.

---

6 | The surveys were funded by the City of Split, in the process of preparing the Draft Management Plan for the Historical Core of Split and the Substructures of the Palace of Diocletian.

Together, these two age categories made up 57% of the sample, surpassing by far the percentage of comparable age categories in 2012 WYSE global survey of international tourism, which stood at 29%.[7]

Furthermore, it has been shown again—just as in the survey carried out in 2005—that the historical core of Split is visited mostly by tourists traveling without children: in 2013 survey, such visitors made no less than 74% of the sample. This is in stark contrast with the tradition of family tourism on the Eastern Adriatic coast and can contribute to the impression that a new (mono)culture of visitors is emerging in the surveyed area.

However, despite the general accuracy of the observations made by the inhabitants of the area, the types of tourists revealed by the cluster analysis allow for a more complex picture to emerge, also with regard to—so to speak—compatibility of visitors with the heritage qualities of the historical core of Split. Namely, in addition to the already cited data on their age and on their traveling with or without children, the descriptions of the types of visitors obtained by cluster analysis also include information on their motivations, education, income and activity on location.

In contrast with the results of 2005 survey, in which cluster analysis yielded three types of visitors mentioned earlier in the essay, four different types were revealed in 2013. The first type makes 22% of the sample and comprises visitors who are "not interested in anything special". Represented above average among them are tourists aged 16 to 35 with the highest levels of educational attainment (including doctoral degrees), or attending secondary education or university. High school and university students from France and Croatia figure prominently in this group, while those from Germany and Great Britain are underrepresented. As regards their monthly income, almost a quarter (24%) of the visitors in this group report it to be between one and three thousand Euros, 20% say it is over three

---

7 | As was mentioned in endnote 4, in WYSE's "New Horizons III" 2012 survey of international tourisms, tourists aged 15-24 made 14%, and those aged 25-34 15% of the sample.

thousand Euros, and 18% that it is below one thousand Euros. Regardless of such differences in disposable income, what is common to the visitors in this group is that they have no preformed expectations but are willing to engage in whatever activities they find to be interesting on location.

The second type also makes 22% of the sample and comprises what can be described as "experiential" visitors. These are culturally motivated tourists, who would like to experience historical monuments and localities, visit places outside the usual tourist routes, and eat in restaurants with local cuisine. They are educated above average, frequently with higher levels of educational attainment (specialization, master's or doctoral degree), and they are mostly employed or retired. In other words, this is the group in which we find a very small number of those currently attending secondary education or university. Consequently, older tourists are well represented in this group, with 27% of the surveyed visitors aged 36 to 55, and 21% 56 and older. Represented above average in this group are tourists from Germany, and below average those from Italy and Austria. As regards their monthly income, almost a quarter of the surveyed visitors in this group earn over three thousand Euros, 21% from one to three thousand Euros, and 19% less than a thousand Euros.

One cannot help noticing that, in terms of their motives for travelling, the visitors in this group largely resemble the pre-2008 backpackers, and—even more precisely speaking—one type of "new cultural tourists" identified in our 2005 survey in the historical core of Split.[8] However, as regards their compatibility with the heritage qualities of the location, they seem to be more desirable even than

---

8 | Six underlying dimensions of motivation were extracted by Paris and Teye (2010), following their online survey examining the relationship between backpackers' previous travel experience and motivations. Four of the motivations (personal/social growth, experiential, budget travel, and independence) were found to be fluid in relation to backpackers' travel experience. The other two dimensions (cultural knowledge and relaxation), were found to be constant in relation to the backpackers' travel experience.

"authentic backpackers" (calling them thus, to emphasize the difference from young party tourists confused with "backpackers" by the local observers).

Actually, as Cohen's article suggests, a frequent criticism of the reported aim of the backpackers to seek "authenticity" in their traveling experience is that they spend most of their time interacting with other backpackers and not with the locals. Likewise, as argued by Ooi and Laing, the rapid development of backpacking has led to criticisms of its potential negative environmental, cultural, economic and social impacts, and has brought into question the supposed sustainability and purposefulness of this form of tourism. Finally, as we are reminded by Schaffer, current research in tourism scholarship argues that authenticity is a social construction. Consequently, it can be said to vary in meaning with each tourist or with specific groups of tourists. In addition to that, Schaffer argues that—approaching the subject from a performance studies perspective—one can conclude that backpacking is a performed activity and that each backpacker is actually "constructing 'authenticity' every step of the way".

In light of such insights, older "experiential" visitors, who share backpackers' travel motivations centered on cultural knowledge and relaxation (as diagnosed by Paris and Teye), in actuality prove to be more "sustainable" in the context of the historical core of Split. They can be said to be more compatible with its heritage qualities, outlined in the initial part of this essay, in that they are focused more on learning about the cultural monuments and the local way of life, than on performing their own status. It could be said that it is exactly by their viewing the local scene from outside, so to speak, that they contribute to the continuation of local life as usual.

There is no doubt that older "experiential" visitors construct "authenticity" just as other types of tourists and other age groups do, but our observations indicate that their intention is more to "experience"

According to the authors, this would suggest that the two latter dimensions constitute the core motivations for backpackers.

local culture than to contribute to it by "becoming a part of it". Rather than "doing what the locals do", they seem to want to feel the local atmosphere from a certain distance, which in effect helps maintain the balance and course of local daily activities. On the other hand, what makes them different from young party tourists, whose activities upset local atmosphere with a special intensity, is their possessing more cultural (educational) and/or economic capital.

In contrast with "experiential" tourists, those surveyed in the third and largest group of visitors to the historical core of Split (making 34% of the sample), are not interested in cultural monuments and localities but rather in what can be described as "self-oriented (cultural) consumption". The "cultural" aspirations in this case are low, though, and are typically reduced to buying souvenirs, handmade artworks and clothes. "Entertainment", and in general "having fun", also figure prominently among their motives for travel. It is seemingly paradoxical that in this group of visitors, self-identifying as primarily "consumers", those with the lowest income are represented above average (45% of the visitors in this group reported monthly income lower than one thousand Euros).

To be sure, this group also includes 31% of visitors that reported monthly income of between one and three thousand Euros, as well as 29% of those that reported over three thousand Euros. However, regardless of the level of income, the cultural (or, more precisely, educational) capital of this group is lower than that in the other groups: represented above average in it are those with community college or tertiary vocational training, as well as with high school degrees. Represented beyond average in this group are also visitors from cruise ships, and these come mostly from Italy, Austria, Croatia and Great Britain. All age categories are equally represented in this group, with approximately one third of visitors aged 16 to 35, one third aged 36 to 55, and one third 56 and over.

In terms of their compatibility with the heritage qualities of the historical core of Split, however, all age categories in this group seem to be equally detrimental. While it is true that they contribute to the local economy by purchasing souvenir-type goods from small-scale retailers, they also create congestion on the edges of and inside the UNESCO-protected zone, blocking the passage to the local inhabitants along their daily urban routes. Likewise, spectacular costumed performances and various staged events are offered as "attractions" primarily to this group of visitors.

However, what is most damaging to the maintenance of the once so highly praised mixture of the heritage aspects of architecture and contemporary urban life in the historical core of Split is the fact that the visitors in the group of "consumers" are actually not paying too much attention to it but rather look for items to buy and carry back home, or seek attractions to be photographed. In other words, cultural monuments are in this case at best viewed as a sort of a stage set or, more precisely, as a background image of a scene featuring the tourists themselves as protagonists.

In contrast with the group of "consumers", whose expectations are rather well-defined, if limited, or with the earlier mentioned group of those tourists "not interested in anything special", the visitors in the fourth analyzed group (making 22% of the sample) report to be interested in "everything". Their age is beyond average, they are comparatively well-off, and on the other hand they are represented below average when it comes to the lowest (high school) and highest (specialization, master's or doctoral degree) educational levels.

In terms of education, this group actually seems to be a mirror image of the first group in which the mentioned two categories (lowest and highest) are represented above average. In the group of visitors interested in "everything", tertiary vocational training, college or full university or art academy education dominate. These are mostly employed and generally middle-class people, 31% of whom are aged 56 and over, 21% 36 to 55, and 20% under 35. They are above average from Great Britain, Spain and Austria, while the visitors from France are somewhat underrepresented in this group.

One should not fail to mention that the visitors in this group also come from cruise ships. As a matter of fact, when cruise ship visitors are viewed as a separate category, it turns out that a full 24% of cruise ship visitors actually belong to the group interested in "everything". However, they—as well as 19% of those "not interested in anything special" and 17% of "experiential" visitors—are overshadowed in this case by a full 40% of cruise ship visitors coming to the historical core of Split as "consumers".

In terms of compatibility with the visitors interested in "everything" in heritage qualities of the visited area, they seem to have—just like their mirror image group of those "not interested in anything special"—a relatively "neutral" tourist impact on the local environment, at any rate when compared with the group of "consumers". Namely, although much less pronounced than in the group of "experiential" visitors, in these two groups motives that can be described as "experiential", at least to a certain degree, are more pronounced than in the group of "consumers". Also, there seem to be far more openness among the members of this group to the experiences that can be gained at the locality they are about to visit than is the case with "consumers", whose motives seem to be the same wherever they go, regardless of the specificities of the locality.

Finally, in order to get a fuller picture of what vistors aged 50 plus can contribute to the sustainability of heritage qualities of the historical core of Split, we present selected socio-demographic data on this segment of tourists and briefly comment on their reported motives for visiting. Generally speaking, this is a very well-educated segment, with a full 37% having university degrees and further 24% specialization, master's or doctoral degrees. The majority of the visitors in this segment are employed (56%), and their reported monthly income is rather high compared to the other segments of visitors to the historical core of Split: 20% make between one and two thousand Euros, 13% between two and three thousand Euros, 11% between three and four thousand Euros, and 11% between four and five thousand Euros.

Three quarters of the visitors in this segment travel without children, more than a half visit with their partner/spouse, and a quarter with friends. One third rent apartments and houses locally, and one half reside in hotels. Like their younger counterparts, those aged 50 and over also predominantly learn about the locality and its specificities from the Internet and friends. If they are not cruise ship or other day trip visitors (31%), they tend to stay in town up to three days (36%) or four to seven days (24%). With regard to their motivation, one can conclude that visits to cultural monuments (92%) and natural sights (82%) are high as motives for travel, as are learning about the local way of life (78%) and the wish to attend cultural events (65%).

Amost all of those surveyed in this segment said they had already visited or intended to visit the most well-known cultural monuments in the area, and a half had already visited restaurants with local cuisine. If among the cruise ship visitors, they visit museums, and if stationary tourists in the area who are also museum visitors, they tend to be especially well educated (36% have specialization, master's or doctoral degrees) and well-off (38% report monthly income over three thousand Euros, especially if coming from Italy or France). Taking all this into account, one could conclude that—in the case of Split—visitors aged over 50 carry the promise of "sustainability" and their willingness to engage in what has been recently termed "responsible tourism"[9] is above average in relation to other age categories.

---

9 | Cape Town Declaration on Responsible Tourism, formulated in 2002, argues that a kind of tourism that should be developed under such name, among other things, "minimises negative economic, environmental, and social impacts"; "makes positive contributions to the conservation of natural and cultural heritage", "provides more enjoyable experiences for tourists through more meaningful connections with local people, and a greater understanding of local cultural, social and environmental issues" (3). In the case of the historical core of Split, the listed qualities of this "culturally sensitive" kind of tourism are obviously in harmony not only with the needs of local inhabitants but also of maintaining what UNESCO refers to as the "outstanding universal value" of a site on its World Heritage List.

Concluding remarks: On the future of aging tourists in Split

As argued by Gössling et al, already a decade ago, in the energy efficiency context, "there is now broad consensus that tourism development should be sustainable; however, the question of how to achieve this remains an object of debate" (417). The same could be said about further development of tourism that would be "sustainable" and "responsible" towards the highly specific heritage qualities of the historical core of Split. To be sure, this does not relate to the practicalities of local organization of tourist flows: a willing and dedicated city government could do a lot in that regard, and rather swiftly at that. What we have in mind are more long term consequences of the situation described in this paper.

In other words, we are interested in what the present sociological snapshot, taken in the historical core of Split in 2013, reveals as a sort of a window on a wider world of heritage, tourism and age. We are aware of the fact that a snapshot, like any photograph, is a record of a fleeting moment, and is taken at a specific place at a specific time. However, we believe that—given the heritage importance of the historical core of Split and the recognizable features of recent tourist visits to this site—the situation we have empirically researched leads to, if nothing else, asking important questions about the future of heritage and "responsible" tourism, which in this case also represents a question about—so to speak—the future of aging.

Discussing the results of our survey and street-level observations, one might be surprised to learn that those tourists who come to the area as "consumers" (i.e. with the intention of buying items and actively seeking entertainment) actually have much less spending money at their disposal (and also spend much less) than those who say that they are not interested in buying things but would rather like to visit cultural monuments and experience the local way of life. One may also be surprised to learn that age categories—in the eyes of the public and in tour operators's perceptions alike—seem to have undergone partly unexpected shifts in both directions: tourists are considered to be "young" all the way to 35, while beginning at 50 years of age they are already perceived as "older" or "aging".

The category in between—middle aged tourists, usually visiting with children—has shrunk to the range of no more than fifteen years (35 to 50)—and, if found there at all—tourists in this age category no longer visit the historical core of Split with children but rather as couples. Likewise, one might find it surprising that truly "senior" tourist were simply not present in our sample, which is on the other hand consistent with the fact that international retirement migration has not really taken root in Croatia so far,[10] as well as with the fact that organized group visits of "senior cultural tourists" happen in specific intervals, not only in high season but also in off-peak periods.

Furthermore, it is easy to notice a growing divide between haves and have-nots in terms of motives for travel and onsite activities, but also the fact that nowadays have-nots also travel and expect to find the content of interest to them in the places they visit. Finally,

---

10 | As agrued by Božić, the strongest pull factors for international retirement immigration to the Eastern Adriatic coastal area could be its attractive natural landscapes and architecturally interesting towns, a relatively good infrastructure, clean water and air, and the lack of industry. Furthermore, in some regions, the prices of real estate are still comparatively low. However, there are also strong stay-away factors, which currently seem to figure more prominently. The first among them can be related to the fact that the climate is not mild enough to allow outdoor activities all year round. Apart from strong and cold northern winds (bora) and periods of rainfall in the fall and winter, another strong stay-away factor is the lack of cultural activities and limited entertainment possibilities in the winter months. Finally, the Adriatic coast is relatively difficult to reach by car from northern European regions, while it is easily accessible from the neighboring and Central European regions.In such circumstances, it should not be surprising that—according to the data provided by Croatian tax authorities—the typical buyers of real estate on the Eastern Adriatic coast are aged about 50 and come predominantly from Slovenia, Germany, Italy and Austria.

certain travel motivation patterns are also discernible with regard to the nationalities of those who travel. For example, Germans are represented above average in the group of "experiential" tourists, and more educated and well-of tourists from Italy and France among the museum visitors.

For a responsible local government, interested in rational regulation of tourist flows, this could mean that various incentives and attractions should be offered to the types of tourists least compatible with (and least interested in) heritage qualities of the historical core, encouraging them to visit places in the surrounding areas and consequently relieving the intolerable congestion the conservation area has been subjected to in recent years during the summer months. Likewise, local authorities should devise and put into practice strategies aimed at attracting more culturally and "experientially"-oriented tourists to the UNESCO-protected area in the fall and winter months. The prime target population in this case would also be those visitors considered as "aging" or "beginning to age" in their mid-50s, but also the hitherto so far modestly represented "senior" tourists.

However, the suggested measures could prove to be effective only in a relatively short term. It could be that—at present—the older the visitors to the historical core of Split are, the more sustainable they seem to be, but the question remains about how this process is going to develop in the future. In two or three decades, the current backpacking or party visitors will also "begin to age", but it is certain that they will not bring to the table the same kind of educational background and cultural interests, experience of the welfare state, and finally the financial means of the current 50 plus visitors. Given the current depopulation trends in the historical core of Split, there is a rear prospect of further growth of social polarization, and with the expected increase in real estate speculation, the UNESCO-protected "living heritage site" could actually turn into a "dead monument", occasionally populated by the rich owners of historical palaces and houses but completely deprived of the local street life that still characterizes it today.

From a conservationist's and culture lover's point of view, such developments would be a tragic outcome of the trends obviously underway in the protected area. What is more, a special problem with them is that they cannot be fully addressed and reversed locally, given the characteristics of the tourist economy the city of Split is currently highly dependent on. At any rate, to be effective, strategies and policies aimed at resolving the situation will have to be very carefully planned and implemented. How to go about them is beyond the scope and mandate of this sociological snapshot: what it has tried to achieve, inspired by Levine's approach to the genre, has been to offer some sociological insights grounded in one concrete example. It is hoped that, in the case at hand, they could be stimulating in the context of discussions of the place of aging in the field of tourism.

Works Cited

Adam, Robert. *Ruins of the Emperor Diocletian at Spalatro in Dalmatia, by R. Adam F.R.S., F.S.A., Architect to the King and to the Queen,* Printed for the Author, MDCLXIIII. London, 1764. Print.

Adkins, Barbara and Eryn Grant. "Backpackers as a Community of Strangers: The Interaction Order of an Online Backpacker Notice Board." *Qualitative Sociology Review.* 3.2 (2007): 188-201. Web. 9 April 2016.

Ashbrook, John E. "Yugoslav Succession, Wars of 1990-1999." *The Encyclopedia of War.* 2011. Web. 20 September 2016.

Beck, Ulrich. *Risikogesellschaft. Auf dem Weg in eine andere Moderne.* Frankfurt am Main: Suhrkamp, 1986. Print.

Božić, Saša. "Posljednja avantura. Europski umirovljenici na Mediteranu" [The last adventure. European pensioners in the Mediterranean]. Public library, Zadar. 11 March 2015. Public lecture.

"Cape Town Declaration". *Cape Town Conference on Responsible Tourism in Destinations.* August 2002. Web. 20 September 2016.

Cohen, Erik. "Backpacking: Diversity and Change". *Tourism and Cultural Change*. 1.2 (2003): 95-110. Print.

Court, Sarah, and Gamini Wijesuriya. "Annexe 2. People-centered approaches to the conservation of cultural heritage: living heritage". *ICCROM*. 2013. Web. 20 September 2016.

Eurostat. "1 in 5 tourism nights of EU residents spent by tourists aged 65". *Eurostat Newsrelease 183/2016*. Web. 20 September 2016.

Gössling, Stefan, Peeters, Paul, Ceron, Jean-Paul, Dubois, Ghislain, Patterson, Trista, Richardson, Robert B. "The eco-efficiency of tourism". *Ecological Economics*, 54.4 (2005): 417-34. Print.

Levačić, Patrik. "Dalmacija u francuskim putopisima (1806-1914)." [Dalmatia in French Travelogues (1806-1914)]. Dissertation. University of Zadar. 2011.

Levin, Jack. *Sociological Snapshots 5: Seeing Social Structure and Change in Everyday Life*. Thousand Oaks, CA, London, New Delhi, Singapore: Pine Forge Press, 2008. Print.

Lord, Gail Dexter. "The Power of Cultural Tourism." *Wisconsin Heritage Tourism Conference*. Lac du Flambeau, Wisconsin. 17 September 1999. Keynote address.

Ooi, Natalie, and Jennifer H. Laing. "Backpacker tourism: sustainable and purposeful? Investigating the overlap between backpacker tourism and volunteer tourismmotivations." *Journal of Sustainable Tourism*, 18.2 (2010): 191-206. Print.

Paris, Cody Morris, and Victor Teye. "Backpacker Motivations: A Travel Career Approach." *Journal of Hospitality Marketing and Management*, 19.3 (2010): 244-59. Print.

Pederin, Ivan (ed.). *Njemački putopisi po Dalmaciji* [German travelogues through Dalmatia]. Split: Logos, 1989. Print.

Pederin, Ivan. *Jadranska Hrvatska u austrijskim i njemačkim putopisima* [Adriatic Croatia in Austrian and German travelogues]. Zagreb: NZMH, 1991. Print.

Petrić, Lidija, et al. "Nacrt prijedloga Plana upravljanja povijesnom jezgrom Splita i Plana upravljanja podrumima Dioklecijanove palace" [Draft Management Plan for the Historical Core of Split and the Substructures of the Palace of Diocletian], *Grad Split* [The City of Split]. February 2016. Web. 9 April 2016.

Riesman, David (in collaboration with Reuel Denney and Nathan Glazer). *The Lonely Crowd: A Study of the Changing American Character*. New Haven: Yale University Press, 1950. Print.

Shaffer, Tracy Stephenson. "Performing Backpacking: Constructing 'Authenticity' Every Step of the Way". *Text and Performance Quarterly*, 24.2 (2004): 139-60. Print.

Tomić-Koludrović, Inga, and Mirko Petrić. "New Cultural Tourists in a Southeastern European City: The Case of Split". *The Creative City: Crossing Visions and New Realities in the Region*. Ed. Nada Švob-Đokić. Zagreb: Institute for International Relations, 2007. 125-50. Print.

Tomić-Koludrović, Inga, and Mirko Petrić. "Cruise Ship Tourism and Heritage Cities in the Adriatic: The Adverse Impact on Urban Identity, Public Space, and Local Flows". *ISA World Congress of Sociology: Sociology on the Move,* Gothenburg, Sweden. 17 July 2010. Conference presentation.

Wijesuriya, Gamini. "Annexe 1. Living heritage: A Summary". *ICCROM*. 2013. Web. 20 September 2016.

Wild Bićanić, Sonia. *British Travellers in Dalmatia 1757-1935: Plus a Little Bit More About Dalmatia Today*. Zaprešić: Fraktura, 2006. Print.

WYSE. "New Horizons III—The Largest Ever Research on Youth and Student Travel". *WYSE Travel Confederation*.

WYSE Travel Confederation. 19 September 2013. Web. 20 September 2016.

Never Too Late to Remember
Cruising the Past in Paule Marshall's
Praisesong for the Widow

Anna Scacchi

> En Afrique, quand un vieillard meurt, c'est une
> bibliothèque qui brûle.
> AMADOU HAMPÂTÉ BÂ (1901-1991)

ROUTES TO ROOTS

Contrary to an imaginary that consigns them to lack of mobility, and in spite of the restrictions imposed by de jure and de facto segregation, ever since the Middle Passage African Americans have travelled across the Atlantic, as well as within the Americas. In the introduction to a recent special issue of *Tourism Geographies* devoted to "African Americans and Tourism" (2013), the editor Derek Alderman recalled "the highly discriminatory history of mobility and hospitality in the United States" (375), but also underlined that tourism industry has underrepresented the presence of African Americans as tourists, erasing their ability to negotiate the boundaries of segregation and racial hostility and travel on the edge of white suprematism. In spite of their invisibility, which has also affected Tourism Studies, where according to Alderman the conflicted relationship of African Americans and tourism remains underanalyzed, "African American tourists are an increasingly important and profitable segment of the travel market" (376).

In the last decades the tourism market has designed tourist experiences specifically targeting US blacks, especially those interested in visiting places connected with their culture and history. The booming of black heritage tourism is customarily traced back to the late 1970s. 1976 saw the publication of Alex Haley's novel *Roots*, relating the saga of the author's African American family from the kidnapping of his ancestor, Kunta Kinte, from his native village in 18th-century Gambia, to Haley's own genealogical research. *Roots* was an immediate success, but even more popular was its adaptation for the TV aired the following year, which brought African Americans and their history of enslavement and fight for citizenship in the homes of many white Americans for the first time. The novel sold one million copies in the first year and the TV miniseries, watched by more than one hundred million viewers in the United States, became a transnational blockbuster, with audience ratings in Australia and Europe almost paralleling those of the United States (Havens 32). According to Vernon Jordan, executive director of the National Urban League, the *Roots* miniseries "was the single most spectacular educational experience in race relations in America" (qtd in Pierson 19). It certainly helped pave the way for the national dialogue on slavery, segregation and racism that would slowly emerge in the following decades. For black Americans it constituted a turning point in their relationship both with Africa and with their history of enslavement.[1]

---

1 | The story of Haley's successful, if largely fictive, search for roots and discovery of an African ancestor had a deep theraupetic and symbolic value for African Americans, since it offered a counterstory to the dominant narrative tracing black poverty back to slavery's supposed disruption of family ties, a narrative popularized by the infamous 1965 Moynihan Report. As Elisa Bordin has recently underlined, "Haley's telling of a two-hundred-years family story, able to trace his first African American forefather back in the 18th-century village of Juffure, has been perceived (and questioned) as an extraordinary accomplishment, in contrast with the general perception of

Roots spurred the popularity of tours in search of ancestral roots.[2] While back-to-Africa travel was not a novelty, due to the importance of the notion of diaspora for blacks in the Americas, the big change was in the numbers and in the social status of the African Americans engaging in heritage tours, who increasingly came from the middle class. Interestingly, this trend soon caught the attention of corporate capitalism and its marketing strategies: in 1994 McDonald's, a company with a keen interest in black consumers, partnered with the Haley Family Corporation to celebrate Black History Month with a nationwide sweepstakes offering winners a 10-day tour of Senegambia, West Africa. The "Adventure to the Homeland" sweepstakes was advertised in *Ebony* and *Jet* in February 1994. The large group that was selected included also members of the Haley family, an actor from the miniseries and two academics. The experience, one that many participants did not have the economic means to purchase, was openly framed by the sponsor as different from average

---

slavery as a history of orphanhood, social death, and in general as an institution antagonistic to the maintenance of family ties" (Bordin 4).

2 | In the last decades heritage tours for black Americans have expanded to include places linked to slavery in the United States as well as the Caribbean. Black Americans are invited to heal the wounds inflicted by the trauma of slavery visiting not only the West African sites where their ancestors were imprisoned before the Middle Passage, but also more accessible plantations and slavery sites in the U.S. south. Heritage tourism in the United States, however, is often a disappointing experience for African Americans: in many plantations the main narrative is still centered on the "Big House" and the good life of its aristocratic dwellers, while the slave quarters are nothing more than an appendix to it, the pain, labor and cost in human lives needed to make that good life possible still silenced (see Halloran; Small, "Still Back of the Big House"). In December 2014, the Whitney Plantation, near Wallace, Louisiana, opened its doors to the public for the first time as the only plantation in the U.S. South with a focus on slavery. See Amsden.

tourism: it was a pilgrimage to a sacred place that symbolized the homecoming of diasporic Africans and the recovery of a lost origin.³

Travel to places related to the history of enslavement has become an important facet of the current memorialization of slavery and the slave trade. In this chapter I will analyze Paule Marshall's novel *Praisesong for the Widow* (1983)—the story of a typical "sun-and-sand" Caribbean tour which turns into a search for roots for the African American protagonist—in the context of U.S. "roots tourism." Slavery tourism involves U.S. blacks of all ages, but seems to be particularly appealing to seniors, partly because tours in the Caribbean and Africa require money and leisure time that younger people do not usually have, partly because of cultural reasons that are also at the heart of Paule Marshall's novel.⁴ *Praisesong for the Widow* is the story of an identity quest that reconnects the middle-aged protagonist with her forgotten personal past and common racial memories, giving her life a renewed sense of purpose as she becomes a keeper of memories and bearer of alternative knowledge. Avey Johnson is a despondent old woman on the verge of retirement, whose cultural alienation is manifested in her middle class propriety and choice of typically "white" leisure activities. A well-off African American widow well in her sixties, Avey is touring the Caribbean on board the ship *Bianca Pride* with two women friends. All of a sudden she desembarks at the first port of call, Grenada, willing to go back to the comforts of her New York home. After years of denial of her black heritage in the attempt to secure economic stability and fight off

---

3 | Stanford professor Paulla Ebron, an anthropologist, was one of the two academics who travelled with the tour. They were not sponsored by McDonald's. For an account of her experience, see Ebron, "Tourists as Pilgrims."

4 | In an article exploring the meanings of roots tourism as a response to a sense of loss and providing coping strategies to counteract feelings of marginalization, authors Carla Almeida Santos and Grace Yan write that their research shows that seniors of all ethnicities are the age group most interested in tracing their genealogy, making genealogical tourism one of the fastest-growing sectors of the tourism industry.

the degradation induced by poverty, Avey unexpectedly engages in a painful spiritual quest for her roots when she meets an old man, Lebert Joseph, who insists they are kin. She accepts the old man's invitation to join the annual ceremony celebrating the ancestors on the small island of Carriacou, which she reaches after a rough sea passage during which she half-consciously relives her enslaved forebears' sufferings in the crossing of the Atlantic. Her search for reconnection with her own and her community's past finally turns her into a visionary storyteller whose task, very much like a West African *jali*'s, is keeping the memory of the ancestors alive among the younger generations.

Prompted by *Roots* and its TV adaptation, slavery tourism responded to an anxiety about cultural transmission and memory that was spreading in the African American community with the disappearance of the last generation who had a direct experience of slavery and the demise of the glorious Civil Rights Movement era. Older blacks who had lived through the 1960s fights for civil rights increasingly envisioned revisiting and coming to terms with a denied past as an act of responsibility towards the younger generations and their growing disillusionment with 'victories' which had failed to bring about real change. Slavery tourism, like the increasing amount of cultural texts rememorizing slavery, from film to fiction to TV series and visual art, emerges then as strategic postmemory, to borrow Marianne Hirsch's notion of imaginative investment with the past by generations coming after the traumatic event, whose lives are nevertheless marked by what they have not directly experienced. Like other forms of postmemory, slavery tourism aims to keep the past alive not as a history lecture but as an embodied experience (Woolfork), and to ward off young people's disconnection with their heritage.

Denied and silenced for many decades in the public spaces and cultural life of former slave societies, slavery has been recently granted greater visibility since, in the words of slavery historian Ira Berlin, "[t]here is a general, if inchoate, understanding that any attempt to address the question of race in the present must also address slavery in the past. Slavery is ground zero of race relations" (3). Institutions in the Americas, Europe and Africa are increasingly aware of the need to build a public memory of slavery and they are funding initiatives, such as the rehabilitation of sites of slavery, the proclamation of memorial days and the construction of monuments and museums, in order to inscribe slavery in their national histories.[5] Although the tendency is to frame the memorialization of slavery in a self-absolving narrative of healing and progress, these initiatives also recognize that the past has shaped the present and envision slavery tourism as a pedagogical action aimed at building a more ethical future.[6]

---

5 | Whereas Brazil and the Caribbean are dealing, albeit conflictually, with the role played by slavery in the making of their national identities and present-day societies, and some European countries are similarly trying to come to terms with their past via lieux de memoire that inscribe the slave trade and slavery in their national history, U.S. public culture is still characterized by a large void for what concerns slavery. While the historiography of slavery has changed dramatically since the 1950s, establishing the centrality of slavery to the history of the United States and to its notions of democratic citizenship and American freedom, a large gap divides "scholarly inquiry and public perceptions" (Foner xiii). This gap is probably one of the reasons why the United States still lacks a national museum devoted to slavery, in spite of having the largest number of museums in the world. The Smithsonian National Museum of African American History and Culture, where slavery is included in the narrative but does not constitute the main focus, opened in Washington, DC, on September 24th, 2016, on the last available slot on the National Mall. The project for a national slavery museum in Fredericksburg, VA, launched in 2001 by former Virginia governor Douglas Wilder, a descendant of slaves, has come to a halt, filing for bankruptcy. See Small, "Social Mobilization."

6 | In November 2006, the UN General Assembly designated 25 March 2007 as the *International Day for the Commemoration of the Two-Hundredth Anniversary of the Abolition of the Transatlantic Slave Trade*. Member States acknowledged that slavery was at the heart of "profound so-

Being a transnational leisure activity that is remarkably different from other types of tourism, both in expectations and affect on the part of visitors, and marketing strategies and expectations on the part of stakeholders, slavery tourism has attracted the attention of scholars from such various fields as anthropology, cultural studies, and postcolonial studies, and has become of interest to the field of Tourism Studies as well. As Saidiya Hartman remarked in her 2002 essay "The Time of Slavery," "the identifications and longings of the tourist, the formulas of roots tourism, and the economic needs of African states shape, affect, and influence our understanding of slavery and in concert produce a collective memory of the past" (758). It has become imperative, then, to go beyond a simplistic understanding of slavery tourism that relies on redemptive narratives of healing and homecoming, in order to investigate its complexities.

DOORS OF RETURN? DIASPORIC IDENTITIES AND THE LONGING FOR HOME

Sites of slavery are contested memory, since they provide narratives that are interpreted differently by visitors, depending on their national origins, age, gender, class, as well as the locale where the "rememory" experience happens and the stakeholders involved in it.[7] As Ana Lucia Araujo has argued, "the promotion of the Atlantic

---

cial and economic inequality, hatred, bigotry, racism and prejudice, which continue to affect people of African descent today" ("Protection of Human Rights" 829).

7 | See, for example, Paulla Ebron's analysis of the differences in response between African Americans at African sites of slavery, who envision themselves as pilgrims and are anchored to the past, and African American college students visiting Southern plantations, whose feelings of anger are geared to the present and are expressed as social and political criticism of the continuing exclusion of African Americans from full citizenship (Ebron, "Which Memory?"). On the different experiences of tourists, tourism oper-

slave trade heritage has been crucial to the development of a West African tourism industry" (145) and, as a consequence, capitalizing on African Americans' diasporic longing for home has produced narratives that reinvent, recreate, commodify and at times manipulate the past, often eliding the role played by Africans in the slave trade and marketing as slavery sites places with a dubious history.[8] These narratives respond to the complex needs of this specific tourism segment, which participates in the exoticizing attitude typical of the Western "tourist gaze" but at the same time differs from it in its framing of the tour through tropes of familial reunion and recovery of a lost heritage.[9]

Since the 1994 launching of the Slave Route Project by UNESCO and the World Tourism Organization, with the aim to break the silence about slavery, as well as to "foster economic and human development and to rehabilitate, restore and promote the tangible and intangible heritage handed down by the slave trade for the purpose of cultural tourism,"[10] Ghana's slave forts have come to dominate U.S. blacks' imagined genealogy, even though the country had a relatively

---

ators and local stakeholders, see Bruner, Holsey, "Transatlantic Dreaming" and *Routes of Remembrance*, Reed, "The Commemoration of Slavery Heritage" and *Pilgrimage Tourism*. On the difficult relationship of African American slavery tourists with Africa and their recent discomfort with the "Roots narrative," see Wood, "What Is Africa to Me—Now?"

8 | See, for example, Palmié 370-372, about the controversy over the Maison des Esclaves at Gorée.

9 | Tour guides, as Ann Reed found in her field research, adjust their interpretations and language "to suit the sensibilities of tourists that demand a narrative of African solidarity" ("The Commemoration of Slavery Heritage" 101) and in spite of the commemorations being framed as a transracial and transnational effort at coming to terms with the past and healing its wounds, African American tourists are often placed on separate groups from whites and offered the homecoming experience that they are after (102).

10 | Accra Declaration on the UNESCO/WTO Cultural Tourism Programme on the Slave Route, 1995, quoted in Timothy and Teye 116.

minor importance as a slave trading region as compared to the Bight of Benin and West Central Africa.[11] The narrative developed in these sites revolves around the notion of return to a lost homeland, which is central to diasporic consciousness. Communication between Ghanaians and African diaspora tourists, however, is fraught with tensions and contradictions because what for the former is above all an economic opportunity, is for the latter an identity quest and homecoming. The intercourse between the natives, who regard African Americans as *obronis*, that is wealthy Western tourists, and the typical "roots tourist" expecting to be received as a lost brother and regarding the travel experience as transformative and sacred, can be highly conflictual. As many scholars have underlined, African American tourists are often disappointed at the welcome-back narrative they are offered, which seems contrived (see Hartman, *Loose Your Mother*; Reed, *Pilgrimage Tourism*; Holsey, *Routes of Remembrance*). Many African American visitors object to the glamorizing of the forts, aimed at making them attractive tourist destinations, and even regard their restoration as an act of whitewashing that attempts to erase the horrors of the slave trade (see Hahn). While they deem a dismal appearance more appropriate to sites of mourning, on their part local audiences are annoyed by the predominance of slavery in the historical narratives of the castles, whose life has of course con-

---

11 | Ghana is a favourite destination for blacks from the United States because it is an English-speaking country and a relatively stable African nation with a long history of cultural and political exchange with African Americans. Since 1957, when it gained its independence from the British, Ghana has become the African nation with the highest number of African American residents. President Kwame Nkrumah, who had studied in the United States and was friends with many black intellectuals and political leaders, launched a brotherhood policy towards African Americans, encouraging them to relocate to Ghana and help build the nation. His socialist ideals attracted the support of W.E.B. Du Bois and his wife, who moved to Ghana and became citizens, Paul Robeson, Richard Wright and Martin Luther King, jr, among others.

tinued beyond the slave trade era, and at the reduction of Africa to the point of origin of Black America.[12]

In spite of the conflictuality of slavery tourism, the return narrative is never really challenged and continues to keep its hold on U.S. blacks' imagination. When Barack Obama visited Africa for the first time as president in 2009, in one of his first mandate's most symbolical acts for the African American community, he went to Ghana. Though he made no mention of the slave trade in his remarks addressed to the Ghanaian Parliament, he visited Cape Coast Castle with his family, and like many other African American visitors passed through the "Door of No Return," and then turned back and pointed to his daughters the new sign hanging on the gate, reading "Door of Return."[13] The sign was put up in 1998, when the first Emancipation Day was celebrated and the remains of two slaves were brought back from Jamaica and the United States and buried at Assin Manso, a site along the slave route. Reentering through the Door of Return has become a ritual, symbolizing Ghana's willingness to welcome their diasporic kin, that tour guides invite tourists to perform, as Cheryl Finley underlines in "The Door of (No) Return":

---

12 | As Salamishah Tillet argues in *Sites of Slavery*, "heritage tourism works as a form of African American exceptionalism that posits and arrests 'Africa' solely as a site of slavery and thereby denies the specificity and contemporaneity of West-African nation-states. [...] These countries, and by extension much of postcolonial West Africa, now loom as the exclusive mnemonic properties of the African American heritage tourist" (97).

13 | Obama's remarks on the visit emphasized the need to remember but also the progress made from the time of the slave trade: "I'll never forget the image of my two young daughters, the descendants of Africans and Africans Americans, walking through those doors of no return, but then walking back those [sic] doors of return. It was a remarkable reminder that while the future is unknowable, the winds always blow in the direction of human progress." On the "Door of Return" see Holsey, *Routes of Remembrance* 188-190.

At Cape Coast Castle, the Door of No Return is often the last stop on the guided tour, a climactic moment where visitors watch in quiet anticipation as the guide opens the door to reveal the expanse of angry sea where enslaved Africans would have been led to awaiting ships. [...]

Finally, as the guide motions to the group that it is time to go back inside, he points out a relatively new sign above the door, visible from the outside upon reentry. In the now-recognizable neat white lettering, it reads, "DOOR OF RETURN." Placed there as a gesture of reconciliation, the guide explains that is meant to welcome back the thousands of African Diaspora tourists who flock to the monuments each year.

As Finley argues in the rest of her article, however, return as an act signifying the healing of the trauma of slavery is hardly possible: "Is the sign simply a marketing tool aimed at the African Diaspora segment of the tourist industry?" In a similar vein, Saidiya Hartman has asked, "To what degree can the journey of the 'native stranger' be termed a return?" ("The Time of Slavery" 759), pointing out the inadequacy of the notion of homecoming to describe what such journeys entail.

In other words, is return possible for African diaspora people? Is home and the reconstruction of a common origin possible at all for the descendants of slaves in the Americas? As historian Robin Kelley has remarked, the nature of the relationship with Africa as home is at the heart of the diaspora paradigm (71). In academic discourse, where the diasporic paradigm for the analysis of black people's experience in the Americas came into extended use in the 1960s, the usage of the term "African Diaspora" relies on Benedict Anderson's notion of "imagined community," stressing the construction of cultural identity "through memory, fantasy, narrative and myth" (Hall, "Cultural Identity" 24) and highlighting the fictive elements of diasporic consciousness, that is the vision of and longing for the homeland, the feelings of alienation, the desire for return. Roots tourism, however, seems to rely less on a figurative understanding of return than on the notion of an actual reconnection with lost origins, that inevitably plays on biology. In this sense, the question posed by Stuart Hall in his essay "What Is This 'Black' in Black Popular Culture?"—that is, whether it is time to go beyond the "essentializing moment," which was instrumental in constituting black cultural identity, "because it naturalizes and dehistoricizes difference, mistaking what is historical and cultural for what is natural, biological, and genetic" (29)—is answered in the negative by slavery tourism.

Is there a way to envision what people of African descent in the Americas have in common in non-essentialist terms? That is, in terms that do not rely on blood and genetic heritage, but rather recognize that blackness is "a politically and culturally *constructed* category" and, as a consequence, make space for the "immense diversity and differentiation of the historical and cultural experience of black subjects" (Hall, "New Ethnicities" 444)? At first reading, *Praisesong for the Widow* seems to sit squarely within a discourse of essentialized African continuity in the diaspora, usually associated with Afrocentric ideologies, which is predominant in slavery tourism's narratives targeting U.S. blacks. Whereas Avey's rememorizing tour takes place wholly within the Americas, in staging the Caribbean and South Carolina as places whose blackness is more authentic because they have maintained strong ties with Africa, the novel seemingly shares slavery tourism's belief in the possibility of reconnection with the homeland and recovery of lost origins. Avey Johnson's trajectory in the novel, indeed, goes from a northern bourgeois space associated with the United States and whiteness, the North White Plains neighborhood where she has moved with her husband in their flight from the chaos of the ghetto, to a culturally rich black Southern space that stands for Africa. The Caribbean island of Carriacou and the Gullah culture of Tatem, an imaginary place modeled on the Sea Islands off the coast of South Carolina, point to a diasporic black community which has preserved its cultural Africanism almost intact.

Avey's, then, is apparently a journey from a racially inauthentic middle-class existence where black folk culture and religion are rejected, to a spiritual reunion with her true, pure black self. Her spiritual journey ends in the rejection of a false identity, a white mask, and the embracing of her authentic black essence. Yet, in placing Africa in the distance—as an origin that is retrievable only as names that can no longer be pronounced properly, fragments of a few songs, and shadows of long-ago dances (240)—and envisioning the protagonist's return as a bridging movement between New York, where Avey will hunt down the oblivious children of the Civil Rights Movement generation with her stories, and Tatem, where she will take on her great-aunt's role as keeper of memories for the younger generations, Marshall complicates the trope of return. As Caroline Brown underlines in *The Black Female Body in American Literature and Art*, reading *Praisesong for the Widow* as a praisesong to authenticity and unmediated African continuity as some black feminists have done, is problematic as it posits an original lost identity "that elides the tensions of the historical past, the present moment, and heterogeneous, often conflicting, forms of cultural affiliation," creating "a symbolic hierarchy of original, authentic African culture and inauthentic, white capitalist/consumerist culture" (118). In the novel home is not Africa, nor the erasure of "Africa" by a white mask, but a mobile, dynamic space connecting different places and identities. As Simon Gikandi remarked in his pioneering work *Writing in Limbo*, what remains of Africa in *Praisesong for the Widow* is "merely the fragment of (an ideal) memory" (95). Marshall's theme being not return but separation and loss. At the same time that *Praisesong* mourns the impossibility of return, however, the novel celebrates the resilience of the creolized identities of the African diaspora in the New World, inviting its readers to engage in the fight against their civic disenfranchisement in the United States.

Memory and a Necessary Distance of the Mind: Surviving in the Diaspora

The cover of the first edition of Paule Marshall's *Praisesong for the Widow* affords the reader a glimpse of the novel's protagonist. A very proper middle-aged woman, recently widowed, Avey Johnson stands propped against a sea landscape at the bottom of the book cover wearing pearls, a touch of pink lipstick, an elegant matching dress and jacket, and a white hat. Relegated to the margins by the imposing title and author's name, which take up most of the space, she looks frail, perplexed and almost unsubstantial. The artist, Judith Kazdym Leeds, a well-known illustrator who also created the dust jacket for Alice Walker's *Color Purple*, managed to capture the *comme-il-faut* quality of the protagonist's appearance and, above all, her feelings of displacement and unbelonging at the beginning of the novel. Avey and her two friends are the only blacks in a group of senior American tourists who are enjoying the lavish food, luxury cabins and halls and exotic sights their money bought and know nothing about the places they are visiting. Neither does Avey, for that matter, since not only is she completely unaware of the existence of a black diaspora, she has also managed to forget much about her own identity as a black American in her social climbing. Urged by her racially conscious daughter Marion to choose a destination where she could learn something important for her, such as Brazil or Ghana, instead of a "meaningless cruise with a bunch of white folks" (13), she had stubbornly stuck to her plan and packed six suitcases of clothes and accessories for her trip.

In spite of the leisure class context framing her first appearance Avey is only a few years away from the ghetto, which she fled together with her husband in order to find economic and social security and resist the degrading force of racism. Aghast at the breaking down of their marriage life induced by poverty, the couple embraced a middle-class ethics of hard work and saving that brought them from the old, dilapidated tenements of Halsey Street, Brooklyn, to the safety of a predominantly white neighborhood. Avey's climbing of the social and racial ladder has meant denying her cultural heritage, her love for black music and dance, her gusto for vaudeville jokes, her sensuality. Above all, it has meant erasing from her memory the teachings she received from her great-aunt Cuney in Tatem, who through the ritual telling of the story of the Ibo Landing—the account of how the chained Ibos, seeing what awaited them in the New World, had walked across the Atlantic back to Africa, a story which she had unquestioningly believed until the age of ten—had entrusted her with a mission "she couldn't even name yet had felt duty-bound to fulfill" (42). In order to become acceptable to her white neighbors she has forgotten her mission and cloaked her blackness, cultural and physical, under a white mask, a protective layer of propriety and self-control. So much so that she often does not recognize herself when she glances at her reflection in a mirror (141). The same white mask she glimpsed on the face of her husband, after his transformation from loving, carefree Jay to hard-working, sanctimonious Jerome.

The novel's title, however, anticipates that Avey's estrangement from her heritage and sense of unbelonging will be defeated, as praisesongs in African traditions celebrate heroes and sing their achievements. The Fanonian notion of white mask is a central structuring metaphor for the novel's narrative, which seems to frame Avey's quest as a successful discarding of her false identity and recovery of her true black self. The text, indeed, repeatedly lingers on Avey's body, describing it as stately and regal, dwelling on its African features, which she hides under fashionable clothes subscribing to white middle-class aesthetics, comparing it to an African queen's or a Dahomey female warrior's. Avey's white mask is threatened by her black body, whose Africanness can be repressed but not erased. And it is precisely because of her body that her voyage back begins.

After a few days on the Bianca Pride, Avey starts to feel "not herself." She has an odd feeling of cloggedness and swollenness, as if she had gorged herself upon the fancy foods offered in the ship's restaurants. She feels uneasy, almost haunted, because of strange visions that keep superimposing images of violence and death on her surroundings. The old American tourists she is travelling with appear to her as skeletons, trying to grab her and draw her into their death-in-life. She is particularly troubled by the odd dream she had about her great-aunt Cuney, with whom she used to spend her summer vacations as a child, and who named her Avatara after her enslaved ancestor. In the dream, the old woman appeared outside her house in North White Plains, beckoning Avey to go back with her to the Ibo Landing, the place where she used to take the child and tell her stories about her ancestor. As she resisted her aunt's command they started to fight, and Avey was ashamed that the whole neighborhood was looking on while they behaved like typical low-down blacks.

When she finally lands ashore on Grenada, she finds herself surrounded by a multitude of loud gay people in festive clothes, speaking Patois and carrying packages, eagerly lining up to board dingy boats. They are heading, as she learns later, for the small island of Carriacou for the annual excursion, where they will participate in the Big Drum dance, a ceremony reconnecting them to the Old Parents, that is, the African ancestors brought as slaves to the Americas. At the harbor, while she is waiting for a taxi to take her to the airport, she struggles against the feeling of familiarity evoked by the Patois, which reminds her of the accents of the people in Tatem, and the friendly greetings from the people surrounding her, who seem to treat her as kin. Like Mona, the protagonist of Haile Gerima's 1993 film *Sankofa*, who shouts "I'm American, I'm not African," when she is grabbed by white men in the dungeons of Cape Coast castle, Avey tries to stick to her status as an American citizen, rejecting connection with these people, but to no avail, as her black body has already begun to take her back "to her source."[14] Her expensive

---

14 | Sankofa is an Akan word meaning "go back and retrieve," and Gerima's film approaches the memorialization of slavery from a diasporic perspective. Mona, an African American woman who is modeling for a fashion shoot at Cape Coast Castle, is confronted by an old African man who urges her to go back "to her source." While visiting the castle's dungeons with other

clothes no longer seem able to contain her resurfacing blackness and separate her from the black diasporic community:

The problem was, she decided, none of them seemed aware of the fact that she was a stranger, a visitor, and a tourist, although this should have been obvious from the way she was dressed and the set of matching luggage at her side. But from the way they were acting she could have been simply one of them there on the wharf. (69)

After a painful night of wake at the 5-star hotel where she stays, waiting for the next plane home—when she recollects the early happy years of her marriage and the racism and economic troubles that made her husband turn into a money-making machine, and she is finally able to mourn Jay's death—Avey realizes that in their struggle to survive they had given up themselves and wonders if there might have been another way:

Couldn't they have done differently? Hadn't there perhaps been another way? [...] Awareness. It would have called for an awareness of the worth of what they possessed. Vigilance. The vigilance needed to safeguard it. To hold it like a jewel high out of the envious reach of those who would either destroy it or claim it as their own. And strength. It would have taken strength on their part, and the will and even cunning necessary to withstand the glitter and the excess. To take only what was needed and to run. And distance. Above all, a certain distance of the mind and heart had been absolutely essential. (139)

A distance of the mind, a divided self: the notion of a belonging that is also at the same time a belonging elsewhere—what W.E.B. Du

---

tourists she is snatched back to the past and sent to an American plantation as a slave. We then follow her fate as Shola, a houseslave abused by her master. She becomes part of a rebellion and when she is killed she flies back to the slave castle, where she joins other members of the diaspora in a ceremony.

Bois had termed "double consciousness" in his *The Souls of Black Folk* (1903)—brings to Avey's mind Aunt Cuney's words about her ancestor's strategy to cope with her enslavement. After watching the Ibos take a long look around and, seeing the suffering that was to come, turn and walk back over the ocean to Africa, "she just picked herself up and took off after 'em. In her mind. Her body she always usta say might be in Tatem but her mind, her mind was long gone with the Ibos..." (39). As a ten-year-old child, at this point of the story Avey had wondered, "But how come they didn't drown, Aunt Cuney?," a question she had never asked before, and had flinched at the sad, disappointed look her aunt had given her. Now her early unquestioning acceptance of the Ibo Landing myth—which according to Western epistemology cannot but be collective suicide, but is a powerful symbol of resistance in black diasporic folklore—comes back, signalling her renewed openness to alternative knowledge and her future choice of spiritual truth over factual reality.[15] As soon as morning comes she starts wandering on the beach, her new mental disposition signified by her dishevelled appearance. Her chance meeting with Lebert Joseph (an obvious reference to the Yoruba god of the crossroads, Eshu-Elegba), who keeps asking what her nation is and to whom she finds herself telling all about her sickness, the dream and her sudden decision to leave the cruise, will trigger a process of rememorizing reconnecting her with the ancestral roots her mind is oblivious to but her body still remembers. This process

---

15 | The Ibo Landing myth, based on a historical event happened in 1803 at Saint Simons Island, Georgia, permeates African American folklore and is a powerful symbol of cultural resistance in black literature. The motif of the return home of enslaved Africans, either by flying or walking back on the ocean is ubiquitous in the African diaspora in the New World (see Powell). According to Marshall, *Praisesong* began when she read about the Ibo Landing in a book of interviews with elderly Sea Islands people who had been slaves, conducted in the 1930s by Works Project Administration employees (qtd in Wall 184).

culminates with the Big Drum dance, which she initially attends as an observer and then joins, "dancing her nation."[16]

In leaving the white tour and its senile participants Avey leaves a journey without meaning, that cannot offer anything besides mere diversion in the way to death and seems to extend life as duration, and embarks on a spiritual journey which will grant her a new life and sense of purpose. Avey's Caribbean journey, differently from the heritage tours to African slavery sites in search for a a mythic homeland, that aim to restore the point in time before slavery, reconnects her with diasporic blacks in the Americas through ties that are cultural and political more than blood-based. By means of a sea passage where Avey suffers the painful experiences of the Middle Passage, her journey shifts the focus on the fact of slavery and the links connecting blacks in the Diaspora rather than on a mythic ancestral home. The novel's ending, with the final recovery of her diasporic heritage, does not include the dream of an impossible return home, but envisions instead her future role in the United States as a spiritual guide for the younger generations, teaching them how to live in the diaspora with a necessary distance of the mind.

WORKS CITED

Alderman, Derek H. "Introduction to the Special Issue: African Americans and Tourism." *Tourism Geographies* 15. 3 (2013): 375-79.

Amsden, David. "Building the First Slave Museum in America." *The New York Times Magazine* 26 February 2015. Web. 21 July 2015.<http://www.nytimes.com/2015/03/01/magazine/building-the-first-slavemuseum-inamerica.html?hp&action=click&

---

16 | On the Carriacou Big Drum and Nations Dance, see McDaniel, which was inspired by Marshall's novel and adopts its four-section structure ("Runagate," "Sleeper's Wake," "Lavè Tête," and "The Beg Pardon"), and Taylor.

pgtype=Homepage&module=photo-spotregion&region=top-news&WT.nav=top-news&_r=0>.

Araujo, Ana Lucia. "Welcome the Diaspora: Slave Trade Heritage Tourism and the Public Memory of Slavery." *Ethnologies* 32.2 (2010): 145-78.

Berlin, Ira. "Coming to Terms with Slavery in Twenty-First-Century America." *Slavery and Public History: The Tough Stuff of American Memory*. Eds. James Oliver Horton and Lois E. Horton. New York: The New Press, 2006. Print.

Bordin, Elisa. "Looking for Kunta Kinte. Alex Haley's *Roots* and African American Genealogies." *Iperstoria* 4 (2014): 3-9. Web. 11 May 2014. <http://www.iperstoria.it/joomla/images/PDF/Numero5/Saggi_monograficabordin_roots.pdf>.

Brown, Caroline. *The Black Female Body in American Literature and Art: Performing Identity*. New York: Routledge, 2012. Print.

Bruner, Edward H. "Tourism in Ghana: The Representation of Slavery and the Return of the Black Diaspora." *American Anthropologist* 98. 2 (1996): 290-304.

Ebron, Paulla A. "Tourists as Pilgrims: Commercial Fashioning of Transatlantic Politics." *American Ethnologist* 26. 4 (1999): 910-32.

Ebron, Paulla A. "Which Memory?" *Transatlantic Memories of Slavery: Reimagining the Past, Changing the Future*. Eds. Elisa Bordin and Anna Scacchi. Amherst: CambriaPress, 2015. 133-59. Print.

Finley, Cheryl. "The Door of (No) Return." *Common Place: The Interactive Journal of Early American Life* 1. 4 (2001). Web. 3 June 2015. <http://www.common-placearchives.org/vol-01/no-04/finley/>.

Foner, Eric. *Who Owns History?: Rethinking the Past in a Changing World*. New York: Hill and Wang, 2002. Print.

Gikandi, Simon. *Writing in Limbo: Modernism and Caribbean Literature*. Ithaca: Cornell UP, 1992. Print.

Hahn, E. Emmons. "The Commodification of Authenticity for Historic Sites." *Cultural and Heritage Tourism* 2012. Web. 1 September 2015.<http://sustainableheritagetourism.com/cultural-tourism/the-commodificationof-authenticity-in-historic-sites/>.

Hall, Stuart. "Cultural Identity and Diaspora." 1990. *Diaspora and Visual Culture: Representing Africans and Jews*. Ed. Nicholas Mirzoeff. New York: Routledge 2000. 21-33.

Hall, Stuart. "New Ethnicities." *Stuart Hall: Critical Dialogues in Cultural Studies*. Eds. David Morley and Kuan-Hsing Chen. New York: Routledge 1996. 442-51. Print.

Hall, Stuart. "What Is This 'Black' in Black Popular Culture?" *Black Popular Culture*. Project by Michele Wallace. Ed. Gina Dent. Seattle: Bay Press, 1992. 21-37. Print.

Halloran, Vivian Nun. "Between Plantation and Living History Museum." *Exhibiting Slavery: The Caribbean Postmodern Novel as Museum*. Charlottesville: U of Virginia P, 2009. 100-20.

Hartman, Saidiya. "The Time of Slavery." *South Atlantic Quarterly* 101.4 (2002): 757-77.

Hartman, Saidiya. *Lose Your Mother: A Journey Along the Atlantic Slave Route*. New York: Farrar, Straus and Giroux, 2007. Print.

Havens, Timothy. "*Roots* and the Perils of African American Television Drama in a Global World." *Black Television Travels: African American Media around the Globe*. New York: New York UP, 2013. Print.

Hirsch, Marianne. *The Generation of Postmemory: Writing and Visual Culture after the Holocaust*. New York: Columbia UP, 2012. Print.

Holsey, Bayo. "Transatlantic Dreaming: Slavery, Tourism and Diasporic Encounters." *Homecomings: Unsettling Paths of Return*. Eds. Fran Markowitz and Anders H. Stefansson. Oxford, UK: Lexington Books, 2004. 166-82. Print.

Holsey, Bayo. *Routes of Remembrance: Refashioning the Slave Trade in Ghana*. Chicago: U of Chicago P, 2008. Print.

Kelley, Robin D. G. "The African Diaspora and the Re-Mapping of U.S. History." *Teaching American History in a Global Context*. Eds. Carl J. Guarneri and Jim Davis. New York: Routledge 2015. Print.

Marshall, Paule. *Praisesong for the Widow*. New York: Putnam, 1983. Print.

McDaniel, Lorna. *The Big Drum Ritual of Carriacou: Praisesongs in Rememory of Flight*. Gainsville: UP of Florida, 1998. Print.

Palmié, Stephan. "Slavery, Historicism and the Poverty of Memorialization." *Memory: Histories, Theories, Debates*. Eds. Susannah Radstone and Bill Schwarz. New York: Fordham UP, 2010. Print.

Pierson, Eric. "The Importance of *Roots*." *Watching While Black: Centering the Television of Black Audiences*. Ed. Beretta E. Smith-Shomade. New Brunswick, NJ: Rutgers UP, 2012. Print.

Powell, Timothy B. "Ebos Landing." *New Georgia Encyclopedia*, June 15th, 2004. Web.<http://www.georgiaencyclopedia.org/articles/history-archaeology/eboslanding>. Web. 3 October 2015.

"Protection of Human Rights." *Yearbook of the United Nations 2006*, vol. 60. United Nations Publications, 2009. Print.

Reed, Ann. "The Commemoration of Slavery Heritage: Tourism and the Reification of Meaning." *The Cultural Moment in Tourism*. Eds. Laurajane Smith, Emma Waterton and Steve Watson. New York: Routledge, 2012. Print.

Reed, Ann. *Pilgrimage Tourism of Diaspora Africans to Ghana*. New York: Routledge, 2014. Print.

Santos, Carla A. and Grace Yan. "Genealogical Tourism: A Phenomenological Examination." *Journal of Travel Research* 49.1 (2010): 56-67.

Small, Stephen. "Social Mobilization and the Public History of Slavery in the United States." *Eurocentrism, Racism and Knowledge: Debates on History and Power in Europe and the Americas*. Eds. Martha Araújo and Silvia R. Maeso. Basingstoke: Palgrave Macmillan, 2015. 229-46. Print.

Small, Stephen. "Still Back of the Big House: Slave Cabins and Slavery in Southern Heritage Tourism." *Tourism Geographies* 15.3 (2012): 405-23.

Taylor, Patrick, "Post-Colonial Encounters: Paule Marshall's 'Widow's Praisesong' and George Lamming's 'Daughter's Return'." *And the Birds Began to Sing: Religion and Literature in Post-Colonial Cultures*. Ed. Jamie S. Scott. Amsterdam: Rodopi, 1996. 191-208. Print.

Tillet, Salamishah. *Sites of Slavery: Citizenship and Racial Democracy in the Post-Civil Rights Imagination.* Durham, NC: Duke UP, 2012. Print.

Timothy, Dallen J. and Victor B. Teye. "American Children of the African Diaspora: Journeys to the Motherland." *Tourism, Diasporas and Space.* Eds. Tim Coles and Dallen J. Timothy. New York: Routledge, 2004. Print.

Wall, Cheryl A. "Bare Bones and Silken Threads: Lineage and Literary Tradition in *Praisesong for the Widow*." *Worrying the Line: Black Women Writers, Lineage, and Literary Tradition.* Chapel Hill: U of North Carolina P, 2005. 181-208. Print.

Wood, Marcus. "What Is Africa to Me—Now?" *Transatlantic Memories of Slavery: Reimagining the Past, Changing the Future.* Eds. Elisa Bordin and Anna Scacchi. Amherst: Cambria Press, 2015. 73-93. Print.

Woolfork, Lisa. *Embodying American Slavery in Contemporary Culture.* Champaign: U of Illinois P, 2008. Print.

Cruising to be Young Again

The Mystification of Senior Tourism in *Love Boat*

Cinzia Schiavini

Cruise ship tourism is one of the first images that comes to mind when thinking about tourism and the third age. Although nowadays the equation seems to be less valid, since only one in four cruisers is retired and the market is becoming more and more family-oriented, traditionally cruising has been (or has been seen as) the preserve of older people (Dowling 5). From the 1970s onward, cruise industry has been the largest growing segment of the leisure travel industry, with the number of passengers carried increasing by 2,200%—from 500,000 to close to 11 million North Americans per year, and with an occupancy rate of nearly 90% (Klein 261; Patterson 131).

It is not surprising that cruise ship tourism found a fertile ground in the United States: the availability of capitals to invest in the tourist industry and the proximity to idyllic seascapes like the Caribbean and Hawaii constituted the material basis of its success. However, cultural traditions and suggestions have been pivotal in the boom of cruise ship as a popular tourist practice. Key factors have been a tradition of ship tourism that thrust its roots in the first transatlantic leisure voyages toward Europe as early as the 1880s; the renewed success of cruising during Prohibition in the Twenties, due to the fact that alcohol could be served outside the national boundaries; the tendency in United States mass tourism, from the Fifties onward, to conceive holidays as journeys—even though, in the Fifties and Sixties, they were mainly automobile journeys within the national boundaries. Last but not least, a demographic turn—the so called "graying" of North America, in the second half of the twentieth century, and the tendency to transform the cultural obsession with youth and the fear of getting old into a multibillion dollar industry, which soon incorporated tourist practices as well.

Tourism, as a paramount case of consumerist performance, was a particularly suitable product of consumption marketed by the media. As Rossana Bonadei reminds us, "Tourism, in its being a performance limited in time and space, concentrates in itself the capitalist spectacle with all its parade of special effects: media support, advertisement imagery, luxury exhibitions, marketing fireworks, 'memorable' events'" (Bonadei 58).

The elderly became the ideal target, and not only because they were a growing share of the market in those years. With a privileged status among welfare-state beneficiaries (at last until the early 1980s) and without mortgages or children to look after, the elderly possessed a relatively large share of discretionary income (Patterson 57). Besides having more money to spend, they had also more time and were more flexible as far as holiday periods; they became more active than in the past and willing to shake off the boredom of everyday routine in search of fun. Cultural representation of the elderly changed too: efforts to eliminate negative stereotypes of and prejudices against older people and depict them as necessarily healthy, sexually active, engaged, productive, and self-reliant (Cole 229) had been going on since the 1960s (see Robert Butler, *Why Survive?* 1975), but it was in the Seventies that third age started to be perceived and represented as a new phase of life, rather than the end of it.

Cruise ship tourism is especially apt to be experienced by third age individuals for several reasons. As Christine Chin points out, "mass market tourism appeals to, and reinforces what Ritzer and Liska identify as the four principles of predictability, efficiency, calculability and controllability that similarly order ordinary life especially of the US middle classes. Succinctly put, cruise passenger-tourists are able to consume new sights and experiences from the comfort and security of a structured 'home' away from home" (Chin 14).

Like the guided tour, the ship has an insulation function for the tourists from the external environment, and it helps to integrate tourists among themselves—the latter a key feature in a leisure activity for a segment of the population that has a high proportion of singles (Van Harssel 367). Cruise ship tourism provides access to places inaccessible by land; it offers leisure and entertainment facilities; it nurtures both the desire for social relations among the passengers' community and a domesticated encounter with the exotic, often to the point of turning destinations into extensions of the ship, while at the same time solving many of the concerns that worry senior tourists. So "[the elderly] are able to visit a succession of foreign destinations without the hassles of coordinating point to point flight schedules with hotel reservations, packing and unpacking suitcases, searching for good local restaurants as well as tourist sites and having to make their own way there" (Chin 2).

Although cruise ship tourism took its first steps in the Sixties (with the partnership between Ted Arison and the Norwegian Company Kloster Reederei to offer Caribbean cruises from the then little port of Miami), until the Seventies it was mainly a regional phenomenon: passengers largely came from the coast, mainly because companies had not enough money for a national campaign and thus most Americans had no idea about what a cruise was. And even though from 1969 to 1971 Royal Caribbean started introducing 700-880 passenger vessels, for most of the Seventies cruising in the American imagination, both in literature and in the media, largely related to wreckships and disasters—as the success of *The Poseidon Adventure* (1972) testifies.

Things changed abruptly on May 5th, 1977, when *The Love Boat* was first aired, launching cruise ship as an affordable fantasy vacation for middle-class, mostly seniors, consumers. The idea came from a book, *Love Boats* (1975), the autobiographical account of a cruise director, Jerardine Saunders, that described cruises as an exotic, funny world of sexual awakening or play. A negative review of the book in the *Los Angeles Times* drew the attention of Douglas

Cramer, a TV producer who was looking for new themes and a setting for another romantic comedy.

Love Boat was the first and probably the only TV series (and one of the very few cultural products in general) devoted to cruise ship tourism; and like its closest counterpart, *Fantasy Island*, and many other serials, it was first introduced to viewers not as a series, but as a movie. However, when ABC required a sequel after the success of the full-length film, a two-hours special (now seen as the Episode Zero, and a sort of bridge between the movie and the series) was issued, with most of its cast changed, except for two actors—Bernard Kopell, playing Doc; and Fred Grandy, playing Gopher. The new entries were the Captain, from there onward played by Gavin MacLeod, a successful actor at the time, made famous by the leading role in *The Mary Tyler Moore Show*; the cruise director, Julie, interpreted by Laureen Tewes—an actress who appeared as an extra in *Starsky and Hutch* and who was at the time making ends meet as a waitress; and finally the black waiter, Isaac, played by Ted Lange, a Shakespearean actor who had already appeared in several sitcoms—and initially opposed by the *Pacific Princess* company, worried that the inclusion in the cast of a black character could impair their appeal to potential customers.

When, on September 24th, 1977, the nautical series debuted during prime time, it was attacked by critics, but the public loved it: fifty-five million households saw it at its peak. Syndicated in forty-seven countries, the series ran for nearly a decade. Sets of writers were hired to assemble different story lines for each episode, usually in what was meant to be a tripartite pattern: a story concerning young love, comic variations for middle-aged couples, and a romance between seniors. Far from originality or unconventionality, the success of the show was mainly due to the cheerfulness of the regular cast and the appearance of cinema and television stars. A "Happy, amnesiac world where the responsibilities of everyday life were abandoned at the gangway" (Garin 95), *Love Boat* embodied fantasies of escape both from the burden of every-day life and, as it will be discussed, from the passing of time.

The chief characteristics of the series were the dream of love (in all its variants—the show pushed sexual boundaries to an extent previously unknown to TV), combined with a family-like atmosphere that reproduced the relationship existing in a mono-parental family, with Captain Stubbing as the "father"—first metaphorical and then real, with the appearance of his eight-year old child. "*The Love Boat* positioned cruising as exoticism wrapped in a security blanket. [...] The crew, with its good-humoured, gently guiding presence, was like a combination of den mother and pimp" (Garin 100). The security blanket, the safe nest, was the boat itself: Pacific Princess, where the series was shot, was a small cruise ship, with a maximum of six hundred passengers—relatively few, compared to the nine hundred passenger vessels already launched at the time and the three thousand and more that megaships can accommodate nowadays.

The success of the show was not related to the storylines or the performances of the actors, but on the idea of democracy it was able to convey: the series brought even the guest stars (not accidentally, they were often old movie stars, grown kinder and gentler, more approachable over the years) back into the real world—a real ship advertised on the newspaper and full of people with whom spectators could identify; a world both exciting and accessible for the audience, who could (and was *de facto* asked to) dream of getting on board. Everything in *Love Boat* seemed to be participatory, inclusive—especially the experience of love. However, this inclusiveness turns out to be, paradoxically, also very exclusive, as far as the golden age and its representation are concerned. And it is precisely this "exclusivity" which can help us to understand the role *Love Boat* played both in popular culture and cultural industry and in the tourist marketing policies of the time.

The first parameter to be fixed when discussing "cruise ship tourism and golden age" is how old is old—when the "third age" begins. However, it is the series itself that establishes this parameter, and right in the third episode, when a group of elderly people, members of the "Life begins at Sixty" club come aboard, escorted by Mr. Right, the tour guide, a charming young man who would like to have a romantic affair with Julie. The second, more complex parameter concerns the regularity of old characters in the episodes, and the resulting representation, underrepresentation (and misrepresentation) of the golden age.

Here the first paradox emerges: the elderly are underrepresented in the series, despite the fact that there are a lot of elderly people in *Love Boat*. What the audience may notice is first of all the discrepancy between the many old passengers getting onboard that appear in the real-life sequence at the beginning of each episode, and the fictional ones, as far as both protagonists and background actors are concerned. This "selective gangway process", where real passengers, mostly old, enter the gangway and mostly young ones are found at its exit, can be noticed in all episodes. Moreover, especially in the first ones, old characters are nearly always only escorting the young protagonists: like the English aunt drinking hard liquors and travelling with the teen-ager nephew from Brooklyn (1/1/3), who falls in love for the first time. Especially at the beginning, these elderly people are portrayed as obstacles to life and romance—from the grandmother who wants to find a husband for her niece (1/2/2) and misdirects her to the wrong person (Doc, a renowned *gigolò*); or even (more comically and less systematically) they try to discourage love and its expressions—like the old woman who hits people flirting with her bag, if they are not married (1/3/1).

The most striking example of elderly people being obstacles to love can be found in the already mentioned "Life Begins at Sixty" episode, the only one (at least in the first two series) in which a tourist group comes aboard: noisy, infantilized, hyperactive and intrusive, lacking individual identities in their matching requests and actions (often performed in unison), these elderly people end up ruining Julie's affair with Mr. Right in their spasmodic attempt to have fun. A fun they achieve to the detriment of the fulfilment of a love affair. The group is not depicted negatively, however; there is no malice or wickedness in their behaviour—just the desire to get the best they can from the short time of a cruise—a sort of epitome of the tourists' attitude. In their final apologies, or, as they say, "explanation" just before leaving the ship, the group's defence of their behaviour to the understanding couple is that "the golden age is all we live—it's nice, but it's dull [...] we are sorry, but we are realistic: you have more time than we do" (1/1/3-44-45.20).

Because of this lack of time (that is quite ironical, thinking about the promise of a "life that begins at Sixty"), and the urge to have fun, the audience would expect in the following episodes plenty of elderly people intent on enjoying themselves abcard a cruise ship. However, despite one storyline out of three allegedly devoted to a romance of seniors, there are very few people who are explicitly elderly, over sixty—approximately a dozen out of more than three hundred characters. Besides, they are often both the most stereotyped characters in the episode and the more distant from the audience the series addresses, or would like to address (white and middle class), from an ethnic or economic point of view. The elderly are mostly immigrants —like the inspector's father, a first generation Polish American who cannot speak English, or the Italian grandmother travelling with a hen to have fresh eggs. The elderly are racially distinct—like the old black man, whose "minstrelling" performances deeply annoy a pretty African-American scholar, interested in Black history, who does not realize, until the very end, that appearances are misleading: African-American history is there, in front of her, the old man being a very famous baseball player in the Black League. Finally, the elderly are poor: like the old couple visiting their daughter and grandchildren in Mexico, who cannot afford the cruise (and they end up being helped by the crew, with a whip-round).

Besides these "others", there are very few examples of golden age: an old man and a woman who were in love during college but who haven't seen each other for forty years (2/1/1): feeling old and inadequate, she pretends to be her own sister; however, he is not misled by her trick, and falls in love with her again. Finally, there is an old lady who decides to move onboard for good with her many antiques (2/1/2), and falls in love with a waiter, on his last cruise before retirement. He wants to leave the ship and she will end up following him (a storyline that is repeated in a following episode, with another rich lady falling in love with her driver, on his way to retirement). However, there are a lot of actors that look well past their sixties in all episodes, but whose characters are more difficult to label as "third age." What makes these ones different from the dozen previously mentioned?

Aging is not only a question of biology; it also has a cultural meaning, and has nowadays become a category of difference. According to De Falco (4), old age makes the subject both invisible and unmistakable, spectacle and specimen, a split subject that internalizes difference. Golden age can thus be a destabilizing element in contemporary Western societies, because it questions people's social identity—especially in industrial societies based on production.

How then can golden age's subversive potential be defused and the elderly re-incorporated in a productive model of society? In *Love Boat* this re-incorporation takes place mainly through the two most stabilizing social categories: work and family. Despite the lack of social bonds a ship guarantees and freedom as far as social identities are concerned, what makes people over sixty younger in *Love Boat* is first of all the role they play not on the ship, but on shore: except for the dozen mentioned above, they have got a job. Not only most of the seniors (or people who look seniors) are still in activity, but they conceive business, sometimes obsessively, as the core of their lives: as in the second episode of the first series, where an African-American sausage manufacturer compulsively thinks and talks about his sausages, both to his wife and to strangers (1/1/2); or as happens with Beverley (interpreted by Tza Tza Gabor, who was then past sixty), the author of "Dear Beverly Column," a popular journalist so much involved in her work, even on holiday, that she does not realize that her husband—Leslie Nielsen, then in his fifties—cheats on her with a younger passenger.

What we can infer is that since the concept of leisure time is conceived as opposed to "working time," without the latter even the experience of the cruise seems to be deprived of its meaning. And even though Beverly pushes the boundary too far, depriving the cruise of its leisure function because of her commitment to work, the message her story conveys is that on the verge of golden age you cling even stronger to your productive role within society, because it is your job that can guarantee to your self-fulfilment, success, the admiration of strangers and a younger husband—if you do not ignore him too much.

Productivity has been for a long time the premise and the requirement of tourism, since tourism and leisure activities in general are functional to work. As Jost Krippendorf argued in his pioneer study on tourism, leisure time "is socially unproductive and hence lacking a purpose or value. Its main socially accepted use is to serve work: to regenerate man's physical and mental capacity for work. Moreover, leisure time is consumer time creating work and bringing in revenue" (Krippendorf 79). The balancing function of tourism is evident: it fulfils the necessity of amusement in a system where deviance is channeled into mock transgression, a relief from duties and productive activities that nevertheless does not break or even question the social contract, but becomes part of it. Since leisure is rationalized with reference to working time, retirement deeply de-stabilizes the relationship existing between work and tourism, and the latter is reduced to a coda of productive practices—a coda in which time runs fast, and you can't waste it, as the "Life begins at Sixty" episode makes clear.

As often happens in the representation or misrepresentation of the elderly, in *Love Boat* the insistence on "core" youthful selves (and thus their usefulness in the productive system) betrays both people's dread of change, and at the same time the incapability of a whole culture to conceive positive alternative identities, outside the working sphere or beyond the stereotype. This is particularly significant in a TV product of the Seventies, a decade deeply scarred in the United States by economic crisis and downturn. But also a decade in which globalization and the emergence of new markets radically reshaped western economies, which since then have relied more and more on the practices of its citizens as consumers rather than as workers. In emphasising the strong link between leisure time and working time, and the rejuvenation function of having a job, *Love Boat* testifies to the difficulties in popular culture to conceive the shift from an American identity based on production to another one based on consumption, as far as models (but not practices, as we will see) are concerned.

As regards the golden age, *Love Boat* thus unveils dynamics that were fully recognized and discussed in the following decade, like the importance of "subjective age", the self-perceived age, based on how one feels rather that how old one is. As Ian Patterson writes, "this desire to obtain the most they [the elderly] can out of their latter years as they perceive that their time is running out suggests that people are continually assessing their subjective age as being different from their chronological age" (Patterson 51).

At the same time, the series betrays a peculiar type of nostalgia, not for places, but for a time and identity that the golden age menaces. When elderly people in *Love Boat* are forced to retire, either they regress to an infantilized stage, or they want their job back. It happens with Captain Stubbing's father, a former captain, who tries to usurp his son's role when he gets aboard for a leisure trip after his retirement. What saves Captain Stubbing (and his job) is that his father falls in love with a *Pacific Princess'* cook who is just about to retire as well, and the couple start to plan a life together ashore.

As the two Captain Stubbings episode reveals, besides work, family is the second main frame used to re-incorporate the golden age into the social net. A good share of people over sixty appearing in the show are crew's relatives coming aboard: Julie's parents, who want to divorce after thirty years of marriage because they are "bored" (insisting on the equation between retirement and boredom already established in the "Life Begins at Sixty" episode); Captain Stubbing's uncle, a tomcat who stalks Julie (a comic variation on the difference between *feeling* and *being* young, with a bitter aftertaste); a very athletic couple from Doc's hometown who metaphorically adopt him (and he will reciprocate by saving the man's life); and Gopher's parents—an exuberant mother difficult to keep up with, and a shy father whose relationship with Gopher is made even more difficult by the strong bond and empathy between mother and son.

All these characters are nearly always infantilized, with the only exception of Doc's "foster parents," whose non-biological bond with the crew member allows a less stereotyped depiction of the two. On the contrary, all crew parents act as if they were younger, and their son/daughter often behaves in that specific episode as if he/she were a child. Whether, as Bruce Berger has underlined, being on cruises is, generally speaking, a regressive experience in the service of the ego (Berger 126), in *Love Boat* cruising also takes the elderly back into a time when they were parents, not grandparents, and their daughters and sons were babies.

Besides the "selective gangway" process at the beginning of each episode and the rejuvenation that a job or a family can grant, *Love Boat* stages also a "from facts to fiction rejuvenation" aboard the ship—that is, from the actors' to the characters'. Actors are often ostensibly older than the characters they play; despite this, they rejuvenate not only psychologically, but sometimes also biologically. In the last episode of the first two series, a couple, after thirty years of marriage (he is around fifty-five, she is supposed to be younger—but the two actors are older) find out they are going to have another baby.

Since the condition and concerns of old age could not be unknown to Hollywood playwriters at the time, the misrepresentations of the elderly in *Love Boat* apparently testifies to the difficulties (and sometimes incapability) to accept and represent golden age as a repository of autonomous forms of individual and collective identities, outside working/leisure time practices. However, the misrepresentation is related not only to the content (the elderly and leisure), but also to the specific format (the TV series), and its role in American society and in consumer culture.

From its very beginning TV has nurtured the escape fantasy of its viewers, and has to some extent worked as a surrogate of journeys. Post-tourists do not have to leave their house to be away from home—TV and videos allow you to escape from every-day life and dream of new lives in new places. This does not mean that virtual escapes and real journeys are separate worlds: on the contrary, especially with TV, the first can be the prelude to the latter, nurturing a desire that from then onward will be waiting to be fulfilled.

At the same time, leisure has been more and more equated with consumption, especially when on holiday—a world where the idea of not being there, enjoying every bit of that suspended time, becomes unbearable to all those who have dreamt of being on a cruise once a week for years. A world where people always want their glass full to the brim, because they have paid for it.

What I am referring to is a sequence of the Episode Zero, the movie-length pilot episode of *The New Love Boat*, aired on May 5th, 1977. Radically different from the ones that followed, much more realistic than the rest of the series, as regards the characters (Captain Stubbing is more authoritative, Julie is worried about her job, Doc is not always right), the setting (more members of the crew appear, as well as many more sectors of the ship), and the storylines, which deal with the meaning of love in key moments of life: from romantic love to physical love and every-day life (the newlyweds); the wish to become parents; love between two elderly people and the approaching of death. The protagonist is Morris Beckham, a generous, old man accepting the third age and death as part of life. He even wishes a death at sea (another realistic detail, due to the high percentage of old passengers) because then he would not be alone, and death would happen while he is still enjoying life. Morris meets a couple who would like to have a baby and a senior woman who falls in love with him, unable to accept the flow of time, and who dresses and acts as if she were much younger. Thanks to her love for Morris, she tries to cope with her age; she changes for him, cuts her hair, dresses more soberly and starts dreaming of a life together. In the end, however, Morris's original desire comes true, immediately after the lady has left Morris's cabin. The news reaches the couple and the lady while they are having a toast at the bar, celebrating another desire coming true: the young woman's pregnancy. After a few moments of bewilderment and sadness, the couple decides to name the boy after Morris, and they drink the toast clinking Morris' empty glass on the table.

It is that empty glass that makes the difference: it reveals the gap existing between *Love Boat* as a movie-like experiment, and *Love Boat* as a TV series, with radically different social and economic agendas and impacts. That empty glass, which from now on will be never left empty, testifies to the shift from "ordinary" audience (for whom that movie was the object of consumption) to potential customers, who had to be kept in the position of faithful weekly consumers and for whom the cruise ship was the ultimate product of consumption. And you can't remind potential customers that they may die, because none of them really wants to. From here onwards, *Love Boat* incorporated and misrepresented the elderly because it addressed them as audience *and* customers, recognizing their pivotal role in the system of consumption that both American society and American economy were more and more relying on, and selling them real and virtual experiences—from cruise ship tourism itself to the dream of rejuvenation weekly staged in the series.

Thus, the different forms of misrepresentation of the golden age should not be conceived only as limits or symptoms of the complexity of coming to terms with getting old, but also as "products of consumption" themselves. Besides selling the dream of Love, the series sold (or at least tried to sell) also a process of rejuvenation that the cruise could guarantee. The "dream coming true" aboard the ship is the dream of being what and how old you feel, rather than what and how old you are. As Van Harssel reminds us, the elderly "do not like direct references to age or its limitations. What they do like are products that help them to be active and vibrant and advertisements that help them look it." (367) This dream was sold with a format—the TV series—whose weekly schedule and long run made it a powerful instrument for orienting people's behaviour and market choices.

However, *Love Boat* did more than presciently seeing the elderly as the ideal target: it was pivotal in turning cruise ship tourism into a mass tourist practice. When the series started, cruise passengers where around 800.000; at the end of it, they raised to three million. *Love Boat* was an active part in this development. It not only launched cruise ship as an affordable fantasy vacation especially for the most appealing segment of the market. As a TV series—one episode a week, for nearly ten years—it was to go hand in glove with tourist industry; it mirrored its interest for a mature market and it employed a wide range of strategies to get hold of it. Like advertising, which from those years onward focused not on facts, but on emotional appeal, *Love Boat* transcended real life in order to make that dream come true: it transformed cruising into a pop icon, and the industry benefitted from it.

Real cruising turned for the audience into a cruise backward in time, for the media into a cruising from reality to dream, and for the cruising industry into the flowing of huge capitals. Third age audience could find whichever variant of the rejuvenation dream they liked: college romance, exuberant fellow companions to escape boredom, even maternity—everything, except reality. That was metaphorically left ashore, before the gangway, in episode Zero, before the journey—first in the media, and then by sea, as spectators/consumers—began.

Works Cited

Berger, Bruce, and Ross K. Dowling, eds. *Cruise Ship Tourism*. Wallingford, Oxfordshire, UK: CABI Pub, 2006. Print.

Chin, Christine. *Cruising in the Global Economy. Profits, Pleasure and Work at Sea*. London: Ashgate, 2008. Print.

Cole, Thomas R. *The Journey of Life. A Cultural History of Aging in America*. Cambridge: Cambridge University Press, 1992. Print.

De Falco, Amelia. *Uncanny Subjects. Aging in Contemporary Narrative*. Columbus: The Ohio State University Press, 2010. Print.

Garin, Kristoffer A. *Devils on the Deep Blue Sea. The Dreams, Schemes and Showdowns that built America's Cruise Ship Empires*. London: Penguin, 2005. Print.

Klein, Ross A. "Turning Water into Money: The Economics of the Cruise Industry" *Cruise Ship Tourism*. Ed. Ross K. Dowling. Cambridge, MA.: Cabi, 2006. 261-9. Print.

Lammers, William W. *Public Policy and the Aging*. Washington: Congressional Quarterly, 1983. Print.

Patterson, Ian R. *Growing Older: Tourism and Leisure Behaviour of Older Adults*. Wallingford, Oxfordshire, UK: CABI Pub, 2006. Print.

Popp, Richard K. *The Holiday Makers. Magazines, Advertising, and Mass Tourism in Postwar America*. Baton Rouge: Louisiana State University Press, 2012. Print.

Selnow, Gary W., and Richard R Gilbert. *Society's Impact on Television: How the Viewing Public Shapes Television Programming*. Westport, CONN.: Praeger, 1993. Print.

Van Harssel, Jan. "The senior travel market: distinct, diverse, demanding". *Global Tourism. The Next Decade*. Ed. William F. Theobald. Oxford: Butterworth-Heinemann, 1994. 363-77. Print.

Contributors

Ilda Erkoçi
Lecturer at the Faculty of Foreign Languages, Luigj Gurakuqi University of Shkodra in Albania. She gained her PhD at the University of Tirana with a dissertation on literary tourism. Her interests include the relations between literature, geography, and economy analyzed from an interdisciplinary viewpoint. Her major academic interests in addition to literary tourism include sociolinguistics and translation studies. She is author to a number of articles and has presented at several conferences.

Simone Francescato
Associate Professor in American Studies and American Literature at Ca' Foscari University of Venice, Italy. His current areas of research include late 19th to early 20th century American literature, the representation of aging in American culture, and the cultural history of American tourism in Europe. His publications include *Collecting and Appreciating: Henry James and the Transformation of Aesthetics in the Age of Consumption* (2010) and a critical edition of Grant Allen's travel-related novel *Rosalba: The Story of Her Development* (2012). He is currently editing Volume XXVII ("The Aspern Papers and Other Stories") of the *Cambridge Complete Fiction of Henry James* with Rosella Mamoli Zorzi.

Ulla Kriebernegg
Assistant Professor at the Center for Inter-American Studies (C.IAS) at the University of Graz, Austria. She studied English and American Studies and German Philology at the University of Graz and at

University College Dublin, Ireland and holds a master's and a doctoral degree from the University of Graz. Her emphasis in research and teaching is on (Inter-)American literary and cultural studies, interculturality, Jewish migrations to the Americas, age/aging studies and US and European higher education policy. Her latest monograph *Putting Age in its Place: Age, Space, and Identity in North American Care Home Narratives* focuses on representations of long-term care institutions in Canadian and US American film and fiction. Ulla is chair of ENAS, the European Network of Aging Studies, and co-editor of the Aging Studies book series.

Roberta Maierhofer
Professor of American Studies at the University of Graz, Austria, and adjunct professor at Binghamton University, New York. Her research focuses on American Literature and Cultural Studies, Feminist Literature and Research, Transatlantic Cooperation in Education and Age/Aging Studies. Roberta Maierhofer holds a master's and a doctoral degree from the University of Graz as well as an M.A. degree in comparative literature from SUNY-Binghamton. She served as Vice Rector for International Relations of the University of Graz from 1999-2011. Since 2007, she has been director of the Center for Inter-American Studies of the University of Graz. In her publication, *Salty Old Women: Gender and Aging in American Culture*, she developed a theoretical approach to gender and aging (anocriticism), and she has published widely in the field of cultural gerontology.

Valeria Minghetti
Chief Senior Researcher at CISET, the International Centre of Studies on Tourism Economics of Ca' Foscari University Venice. She has a 20-year experience with teaching, researching and writing on tourism subjects and has worked on a number of projects for important national and international organisations (EUROSTAT, EC, UNWTO, etc.). Her main research interests include: tourism demand analysis and forecasting; the impacts of tourism at local level, sustainability and responsibility in tourism, IT innovation in tourism.

Maricel Oró-Piqueras

Assistant Professor at the Department of English and Linguistics, Univerity of Lleida (Spain). She is also a member of the research group Dedal-lit since it started to work on the representation of fictional images of ageing and old age in 2002. In 2007, she defended her PhD thesis entitled "Ageing Corpcrealities in Contemporary English Fiction: Redefining Stereotypes", which was published in book format by Lap Lambert in 2011. She is currently conducting research on British contemporary writers such as Penelope Lively, Julian Barnes and Deborah Moggach, and on the portrayal of ageing and old age in TV series. She has published her research in journals such as *Journal of Aging Studies* and *Odisea*. She has recently co-edited the volume *Serializing Age: Ageing and Old Age in TV Series* (Transcript 2016) with Anita Wohlmann.

Mirko Petrić

Senior lecturer in cultural sociology, cultural studies, and qualitative methodology at the Department of Sociology, University of Zadar (Croatia). He was the leader of the Sccial Processes and Urban Cultural Policy Working Group, carrying out large-scale empirical research in the process of preparing the draft management plan for the UNESCO-protected historical core of the city of Split (2012-2016).

Ivan Puzek

University assistant in quantitative research methods at the Department of Sociology, University of Zadar (Croatia). He has worked in public opinion research agencies and participated in several academic research projects. He was in charge of the surveys carried out in the in the process of preparing the draft management plan for the UNESCO-protected historical core of the city of Split (2012-2016).

Anna Scacchi

Associate Professor in American Literature at the University of Padua, Italy. Her areas of research include language politics and ideologies, gender and race studies, and autobiography. She has published extensively on the ideology of American English, B. Franklin, H. Melville, W.E.B. Du Bois, nineteenth- and twentieth-century women writers, and Charlotte P. Gilman. Among her most recent books are *Recharting the Black Atlantic* (coedited with A. Oboe, Routledge 2008), *Parlare di razza. La lingua del colore tra Italia e Stati Uniti* (coedited with T. Petrovich Njegosh, ombre corte 2012), and *Transatlantic Memories Of Slavery: Re-imagining the Past, Changing the Future* (coedited with Elisa Bordin, Cambria Press 2015).

Cinzia Schiavini
Postdoctoral research fellow at the University of Chieti-Pescara. She has published essays on Henry Roth, Jerome David Salinger, Herman Melville, Edgar Allan Poe, Mark Twain, Tennessee Williams and on contemporary travel writers and nature writers.

She is the author of *Strade d'America. L'autobiografia di viaggio statunitense contemporanea* (Shake 2011), and *Leggere Twain* (Carocci, 2013). Together with Mario Maffi, Cinzia Scarpino and Massimo Sostene Zangari, she co-authored *Americana. Storie e culture degli Stati Uniti dalla A alla Z* (Il Saggiatore, 2012) and, with Scarpino and Zangari, *Letteratura degli Stati Uniti: percorsi e protagonisti, 1945-2013* (Odoya, 2014-forthcoming). She is a member of the editorial board of *Ácoma. Rivista internazionale di studi nordamericani.*

Inga Tomić-Koludrović
Inga Tomić-Koludrović is senior research fellow at the Institute of Social Sciences Ivo Pilar—Regional Center Split. Prior to this position she was Professor and Head of the Department of Sociology, University of Zadar (Croatia). Her research interests are in the fields of sociological theory, sociology of women and youth, and development sociology. She was principal investigator in several nationally and internationally funded research projects and also participated as an advisor and researcher in the process of preparing the draft management plan for the UNESCO-protected historical core of the city of Split (2012-2016).

Cultural Studies

Gundolf S. Freyermuth
Games | Game Design | Game Studies
An Introduction
(With Contributions by André Czauderna,
Nathalie Pozzi and Eric Zimmerman)

2015, 296 p., pb.
19,99 € (DE), 978-3-8376-2983-5
E-Book
PDF: 17,99 € (DE), ISBN 978-3-8394-2983-9

Suzi Mirgani
**Target Markets – International Terrorism Meets
Global Capitalism in the Mall**

2016, 198 p., pb.
29,99 € (DE), 978-3-8376-3352-8
E-Book: available as free open access publication
ISBN 978-3-8394-3352-2

Martina Leeker, Imanuel Schipper, Timon Beyes (eds.)
Performing the Digital
Performativity and Performance Studies in Digital Cultures

2016, 304 p., pb.
29,99 € (DE), 978-3-8376-3355-9
E-Book: available as free open access publication
ISBN 978-3-8394-3355-3

**All print, e-book and open access versions of the titles in our list
are available in our online shop www.transcript-verlag.de/en!**

Cultural Studies

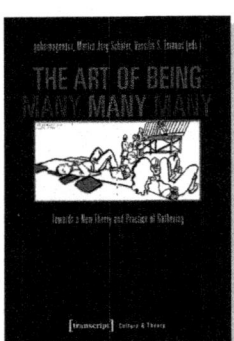

geheimagentur, Martin Jörg Schäfer, Vassilis S. Tsianos (eds.)
The Art of Being Many
Towards a New Theory and Practice of Gathering

2016, 288 p., pb., numerous ill.
34,99 € (DE), 978-3-8376-3313-9
E-Book
PDF: 34,99 € (DE), ISBN 978-3-8394-3313-3

Ramón Reichert, Annika Richterich, Pablo Abend,
Mathias Fuchs, Karin Wenz (eds.)
Digital Culture & Society
Vol. 1, Issue 1 — Digital Material/ism

2015, 242 p., pb.
29,99 € (DE), 978-3-8376-3153-1
E-Book
PDF: 29,99 € (DE), ISBN 978-3-8394-3153-5

Ramón Reichert, Annika Richterich, Pablo Abend,
Mathias Fuchs, Karin Wenz (eds.)
Digital Culture & Society (DCS)
Vol. 2, Issue 2/2016 — Politics of Big Data

2016, 154 p., pb.
29,99 € (DE), 978-3-8376-3211-8
E-Book
PDF: 29,99 € (DE), ISBN 978-3-8394-3211-2

**All print, e-book and open access versions of the titles in our list
are available in our online shop www.transcript-verlag.de/en!**